University of Cambridge Department of Applied Economics

PAPER IN INDUSTRIAL RELATIONS AND LABOUR 6

THE ACTIVE TRADE UNIONIST

A study of motivation and participation at branch level

The Active Trade Unionist

A study of motivation and participation at branch level

PATRICIA FOSH

Lecturer in Industrial Sociology, Imperial College of
Science and Technology

CAMBRIDGE UNIVERSITY PRESS

CAMBRIDGE
LONDON   NEW YORK   NEW ROCHELLE
MELBOURNE   SYDNEY

Published by the Press Syndicate of the University of Cambridge
The Pitt Building, Trumpington Street, Cambridge CB2 1RP
32 East 57th Street, New York, NY 10022, USA
296 Beaconsfield Parade, Middle Park, Melbourne 3206, Australia

First published 1981

Printed in Great Britain at the University Press, Cambridge

British Library Cataloguing in Publication Data

Fosh, Patricia
The active trade unionist. – (University of
Cambridge. *Department of Applied Economics.*
Papers in industrial relations and labour; 6).
1. Trade-unions – Great Britain
I. Title   II. Series
331.87'2   HD6664   80-41538

ISBN 0 521 23700 9

CONTENTS

v

LIST OF FIGURES AND TABLES

ACKNOWLEDGEMENTS

This book is based upon work undertaken for a doctoral thesis at the University of Cambridge. I would like to thank Mr J.H. Goldthorpe, Dr R.M. Blackburn and Dr G.K. Ingham for their help with the original fieldwork. For advice on the major revision of the work since then I would like to thank Professor H.A. Turner.

My greatest thanks go to the BISAKTA branch members at the Sheffield/ Rotherham steelworks, where I carried out my survey, for so patiently answering all my questions; and above all to the two branch secretaries who must remain unnamed. My thanks are also, of course, extended here to the management of BSC, particularly to the managers of the Steelworks Melting Shop and Bloom and Billet Mill.

ABBREVIATIONS

ESC	English Steel Corporation
BSC	British Steel Corporation
BISAKTA	British Iron and Steel and Kindred Trades Association
ISTC	Iron and Steel Trades Confederation
ACTSS	Association of Clerical, Technical and Supervisory Staffs
AEU	Amalgamated Engineering Union
APEX	Association of Professional, Executive, Clerical and Computer Staff
AUBTW	Amalgamated Union of Building Trade Workers
AUEW	Amalgamated Union of Engineering Workers
ETU	Electrical Trades Union
NALGO	National and Local Government Officers' Association
NUGMW	National Union of General and Municipal Workers
NUR	National Union of Railwaymen
TGWU	Transport and General Workers' Union
UPW	Union of Post Office Workers

INTRODUCTION

A great deal of concern has been shown by industrial researchers, management, the media and the unions themselves over the low level of participation in trade unions in Britain, both blue and white-collar. It has been argued that we should be particularly concerned with democracy in trade unions because 'they represent a long history of protest against those elements in the established order which seek to deny to the common man his democratic rights, whether economic or social' (Barber 1950, p.500). On the other hand, many commentators have been anxious lest unions fall under the control of minority groups or interests. In particular, concern has been expressed over the low level of participation at the 'grass roots' level of trade unionism, the trade union branch, where normal figures of attendance at branch meetings seldom rise above 20 per cent and are frequently much lower. Goldstein (1952, p.269) described the TGWU branch he studied as 'an oligarchy parading in democracy's trappings'.

However, low participation in trade union branches is a recurrent and inevitable structural phenomenon since this participation usually involves 'costs' to the individual's other roles, such as familial and leisure ones. This is particularly so since many of the branch activities are concerned with routine detail, while the major decisions are taken at the union's head office. Low rates of participation are common not only to trade union local organisations in many other countries but also to many other types of voluntary associations.[1] We can also note here that low branch participation is by no means a new phenomenon: for instance, see the remarks made by Tom Mann in the 1870s, quoted by the Webbs (1902) together with their own comments about the 1890s.[2]

The far more interesting problem thus becomes that of *who* in fact does participate in the union branch, *why* these people are prepared to sacrifice their spare time, and *how* they differ from their fellow members in their views on trade unionism, politics and life in general. It is particularly important to consider the social characteristics and motivations of these local leaders since plant bargaining and shop-steward movements appear to be playing an increasing role in British industrial relations, accompanied at the same time by increased conflict, apparent separation of interests, and communication problems between the local union leaders and the union head office.

This problem has not been specifically investigated in Great Britain before.[3] Goldstein's highly criticised book of the 1950s was concerned with branch apathy, not with branch activity. And the more recent works on trade unionism in other specific unions, such as those by Moran (1974), Reiner (1978) and Batstone *et al.*

1

(1977), were not designed specifically to investigate the problem of activism, only including short sections on the characteristics of active members. Moreover, these works have a number of limitations of their own. Thus Moran and Reiner both have very small samples of active members (13 and 19 respectively), while Batstone *et al.* concern themselves specifically with shop stewards, and do not systematically contrast the views and characteristics of their shop stewards with those of the rank-and-file.

Nor has there been any specific substantial investigation in any other industrialised country in Western Europe.[4] However, local activism was a controversial and widely discussed issue in the USA in the 1950s and a great deal of research was undertaken there, some sociologists trying to show in an era of MacCarthyism and the 'Cold War' that local actives were not malcontents but 'solid citizens', others (rather less methodically) perceiving local actives as Communist Party sympathisers. Spinrad summarised the more sensible of this material in an article in 1960, after which nearly all of the interest in local participation died out.[5]

Since there has been so little British work on local trade union activism, and since the US material has been so widely referred to in British writing on trade unionism, Chapter 1 begins with a review of the major US theories of local activism, despite the considerable differences between the two countries in terms of the development of their respective labour movements and in the relationship that pertains between their labour movements and left-wing political parties. This chapter also suggests what kind of empirical research on blue-collar activism – which in view of the limited resources available was selected as the focus of the research – was needed to test these theories.

Next, Chapter 2 describes the participation survey that was carried out on the two blue-collar branches selected for the study, in order to identify the active and inactive groups. Chapter 3 considers the relation of the findings of the more detailed interview survey to the assertions of the prevailing theories on trade union activism, while Chapter 4 argues that the local active is rather differently motivated than these theories propose; Chapter 5 considers the sources of such motivation.

Chapter 6 develops a model of blue-collar participation for the two branches selected for the present research, and shows how an assortment of material available in Great Britain from studies of shop stewards and workshop relations, of occupational communities, of other unions and industries and even of political activism, can be systematically collected and pieced together to offer considerable support to the proposed model. In Chapter 7 the wider applicability in Great Britain of the derived model of blue-collar branch activism is considered, as is finally its relation to other more general models of grass-roots trade unionism.

1

A REVIEW OF THEORIES OF LOCAL ACTIVISM IN THE USA

In the wide variety of literature sources that are considered in this chapter, there has been no consistent definition of participation. In fact, a number of differing measures have been used, ranging from simple meeting attendance to specially constructed participation indices. Part of the literature is basically concerned with describing the attitudes and activities of trade union officials and this only provides a comparison between the social characteristics of office-holding branch members and those of rank-and-file members. Because of this variety in the definition of participation and also because of the wide variety of industries and occupations covered by the literature and the fact that a few studies do not distinguish between manual and non-manual workers, the findings of the different studies are not always easy to compare and it becomes difficult to build a general model of participation.

The building up of a general model of participation from the sources in the literature is also restricted by the poor quality (or sheer lack) of empirical evidence in general. Many authors do not present any empirical evidence to substantiate their assertions and make no attempt to quantify their findings. Only a few, notably Form and Dansereau (1957), Wilensky (1956) and Tannenbaum and Kahn (1958) conduct tests of significance: a procedure which is absolutely basic to serious sociological empirical research, especially since the authors who do quantify their findings tend to quote them as percentages. It is only the rare exception who uses any strength of association measures.[1] In this review of the literature, serious consideration has been given only to those authors who produce adequate empirical backing for their assertions.

Theories stressing extrinsic ends

The theory that the active trade unionist has a coherent and articulate political philosophy and sympathises with, and very possibly actively supports, a radical political sect, viewing the union as a vehicle for promoting the revolutionary social change consistent with his ideology, was frequently made in the 1950s during the 'Cold War' and MacCarthyism era and is, indeed, still made to some extent today. The view of the trade union activist as a political extremist has been put forward in the USA by Barber (1950, pp.502–4) in his general article on apathy in voluntary associations, by Purcell (1953A, pp.213–5) in his study of Chicago meat-packing workers, in the case of the 'ideological unionist' by Seidman et al. (1958, pp.242–3) in their study of miners, plumbers, steelworkers, metal workers, knitting mill workers and telephone workers in the Midwest and, in the case of the 'ideological leader', by Chinoy (1953, pp.165–7) in his study of car workers also in the Midwest. In Great

Britain, this view has been put forward by Galenson (1961, p.47) in his very general-ised commentary on British trade unions, by Clegg (1954, p.117) in his study of the NUGMW, by Goldstein (1952, pp.202—9) in his study of a London branch of the TGWU and, more recently, by Ferris (1972, Chapter 6) in his journalistic study of trade union militancy. The theory that a close relationship exists between trade union activism and Communism has also a modicum of vociferous popular support.[2] However, most of these American and British writers fail to provide convincing evidence in support of their claims. Only Goldstein in fact produces any empirical data and his sample was very small.[3] On the other hand, Denver and Bochel's (1973, pp.66—7) work on political activism in Durham offers some evidence that the ob-verse of this relationship holds: they show that their Communist party members were significantly more likely to be trade union members and attend union meetings than their Labour Party actives or their Labour Party voters. Perhaps the most plausible conclusion to draw here is that a very small minority of trade union actives, in Britain at any rate, are Communist Party members or sympathisers and, since they are likely to be hardworking and competent, they will not infrequently be found in positions of authority in the branch (Allen 1957, p.279).[4] However, what Com-munist Party members there are in British trade unions appear to be concentrated in certain unions, industries and regions (Taylor 1974). Thus it seems unlikely that a model of participation based on political extremism will be of general relevance to any investigation into British blue-collar trade unionism. Were participation patterns in France or Italy (where trade unions and the Communist Party can be closely interlinked) to be investigated, the conclusion might be different (Mann 1973, pp. 34—8).[5]

A considerable amount of research into trade union activism was undertaken in the USA in the 1950s to disprove the 'political agitator' theory of trade union activism. However, most of the investigators, while rejecting political motivation, retained the concept that activists were seeking ends that were external to trade unionism — although the emphasis switched to individual extrinsic ends rather than group extrinsic ends. The most widely and consistently expounded theory put for-ward in the US literature at this time was the 'stake-in-the-job' theory. The major proponents were Tannenbaum and Kahn (1958), in their study of four locals in the light manufacturing sector in Michigan, and Dean (1954A, 1954B) in her study of three locals of factory workers in New York state.

According to the 'stake-in-the-job' theory, the active has a 'higher job stake' than the inactive member. This high stake springs from the active's tendency to outrank the inactive in pay/skill (Sayles and Strauss 1967, pp.81—4; Tannenbaum and Kahn 1958, p.96; Kyllonen 1951, pp.528—9; Seidman et al. 1958, pp.170—1; Purcell 1953A, p.206) and in seniority (Dean 1954B, p.51; Tannenbaum and Kahn 1958, pp.97—9; Sayles and Strauss 1967; p.83; Seidman et al. 1958, p.170). The active also tends to be older (Tannenbaum and Kahn 1958, pp.115—6; Lipset et al. 1956, pp. 89—90), male (Kornhauser et al. 1956, p.153; Rose 1952, pp.167—70; Seidman et al. 1958, p.171; Sayles and Strauss 1967, pp.125—7) and married (Tannenbaum and Kahn 1958, p.75): factors which contribute further to his high stake. The active's higher status also accounts for his two further prominent characteristics: (1) his high degree of job satisfaction (Form and Dansereau 1957, pp.7—8; Dean 1954B, p.51; Seidman et al. 1958, p.176), demonstrated in particular by his having a greater number of friends in the plant than the inactive member (Dean 1954A, pp. 533–5; Tannenbaum and Kahn 1958, pp.78–81);[6] (2) his cooperative attitude to management which reflects his greater involvement in and dependence on the company (Dean 1954A, pp.533-5 and 1954B, pp.56–8; Purcell 1953B, p.1276; Tannenbaum and Kahn 1958, pp. 133–142).[7] Thus according to the 'stake-in-the-job' theory it appears that the active unionist is not a malcontent but instead is a respectable citizen akin to the 'pillar of the church' in a typical small town in the USA (Dean 1954B, pp.52, 58).

Dean (1954B, pp.51–56) combines three of these characteristics: seniority in the company, satisfaction with the work tasks performed and amount seen of workmates in leisure time, to form the concept of 'social integration'. This composite variable she found correlated more highly with union meeting attendance than any one of its components singly. She describes this concept as the underlying basis for participation in locals with harmonious management union relations, since it provides 'the feeling of personal identification and responsibility that promotes actual participation'.

The link between the active's high job stake and his union participation is his perception of the primary function of the union as protecting and enhancing his rights to his valuable job;[8] in particular he sees the processing of grievances as central in preventing threats to his job.[9] The higher the member's stake, the more interest he has in shaping union policies and action and therefore the more part he will take in union affairs.

From the relationship postulated by the 'stake-in-the-job' theorists between activity and general satisfaction arose the further concept of 'dual allegiance': the tendency for favourable feelings towards the union to be accompanied by favourable feelings towards the management or company, with the workers perceiving no conflict of interest between the two institutions (Dean 1954A, pp. 531–3; Rose 1952, pp.151–69; Kerr 1953, p.1274–6; Purcell 1953A, pp.531–5 and 1953B, p.1277). Thus if the member considers his wages, working conditions and job security to be satisfactory, he will tend to have favourable opinions of both the union and the management; if he does not consider these factors to be satisfactory, the member will tend to be dissatisfied with both. Dean (1954A, pp.533–5; see also Purcell 1953B, p.1277) goes on to maintain that union members with dual allegiance participate more frequently in the local than other workers under conditions of harmonious company-union relations, but that pro-union, anti-management workers are more likely to attend under conditions of hostile company-union relations.

There are several criticisms that can be made of the 'stake-in-the-job' theory as set out by its major proponents. The specific contentions of the 'stake-in-the-job' theory have not, by any means, been indisputably established by the US theorists. In fact, the only contentions that have *not* been seriously disputed are those referring to the relationship between activity and the factors of job satisfaction,[10] dual allegiance[11] and, to a more limited extent, attitude towards management.[12] The evidence on the contentions concerning pay/skill,[13] seniority,[14] age[15] and sex[16] is contradictory and the support for the marital status contention[17] is only partial. Perhaps most damning is the failure of these theorists to investigate the active and inactive members' perception of the role of the union.[18]

However, the 'stake-in-the-job' theorists' findings both on the relationship between activity and job satisfaction and on the relationship between activity and dual allegiance (in fact, the two relationships which the theorists have most successfully demonstrated) can be challenged on methodological and inferential grounds. With respect to the measurement of job satisfaction, at least some of the 'stake-in-the-job' theorists can be criticised first of all here, for asking too direct questions on job satisfaction.[19] As Blauner (1960, p.355) has noted, a worker in present-day industrial society, where work is so important a part of oneself, finds it difficult to admit that he dislikes his job since 'to demean one's job is to question one's very competence as a person'.[20] This suggests that differences in degree of job satisfaction found in the USA between active and inactive members must be treated with caution, since the factor being measured may be in fact strength of self respect. Secondly the 'stake-in-the-job' theorists can be criticised for having too simplistic a conception of job satisfaction. It is argued here that job satisfaction has many different facets, each of which is a variable in its own right and on each of which a worker may be satisfied or dissatisfied. Workers replying to the question 'Do you like your job?' may be replying in terms of widely different frameworks, some referring to one aspect of job satisfaction, some to another.[21] Again, while Dean does specify the aspect of job satisfaction she is concerned with – actual job operations – she only considers this one aspect and ignores other aspects such as satisfaction with pay or working conditions. The third criticism here is that the 'stake-in-the-job' theorists seriously neglect the question of job expectations in their measurement of union members' job satisfaction. These writers implicitly assume that workers enter the work situation with some kind of identical, fixed and unspecified need for job satisfaction. But it is argued here that job satisfaction cannot be usefully considered unless the varying and individual job expectation of each worker is established first.[22] The worker's job expectation is not a simple single variable but again, like job satisfaction, it is many-faceted and each individual's expectation of any particular aspect of his job may be high or low. Therefore the task of the sociologist in establishing the job satisfaction of a worker must first be to measure the worker's expectation of each separate aspect of his job and then to measure his satisfaction on that aspect. If a worker experiences satisfaction on aspects of his job which he considers to be particularly important, he is likely to be satisfied in general with his job, even if he experiences severe dissatisfaction on other aspects considered less important. Conversely, a worker who does not experience satisfaction in areas he considers important is likely to be dissatisfied with his job in general, even if he experiences satisfaction in other less important directions.

The criticism of the 'stake-in-the-job' theorists' findings on the relationship between job satisfaction and activity on inferential grounds is that there are more convincing and feasible explanations of the empirical relationship discovered by these authors between activity and having a greater number of work friends, than that of regarding it, as the 'stake-in-the-job' theorists do, as an indication of the active's satisfaction with his work situation. As we shall see later, the relationship can also be a product of the active's greater social drive; it can also be a *result* of the active's participation.

The relationship found by the 'stake-in-the-job' theorists between activity and dual allegiance can be criticised on methodological grounds on two particular issues. First of all, the definitions of allegiance to employers and to unions vary between authors: some emphasise 'fairness', while others emphasise the interest shown by the company in maintaining good conditions for the workers. Furthermore, the definitions used are superficial: allegiance to a company or union should consist of more than merely workers' assessments of 'competence' or 'fairness'. Substantial considerations such as, in the case of company allegiance, readiness to leave the company, attitude towards and indulgence in absenteeism and identification with the firm and its products and, in the case of union allegiance, considerations such as supporting union decisions, identification with the union and respecting picket lines, should be taken into account. Secondly, there is the problem of deciding which level of the organisation is to be the recipient of the allegiance: in the case of company allegiance, this could, for example, be the top management or the shop management; in the case of union allegiance this could refer to the shop, the local or the national union. The important point here is that allegiance to one level of an organisation does not imply allegiance to any other.[23] The correlation between allegiances to two different institutions, with each one having two or more levels of potential allegiance, presents a more complicated pattern of interaction than the simple concept of dual allegiance, as expressed by the US authors, can sustain.

As well as methodological and inferential criticisms of the positive findings of the 'stake-in-the-job' theorists on the relationship between job satisfaction and dual allegiance on the one hand and activity on the other, there are also theoretical criticisms that can be made of this theory. Thus it must be noted that the 'stake-in-the-job' theory has been very largely put forward by writers in the USA and it consequently reflects some of the preoccupations of American sociologists; in particular the concept of dual allegiance is unfamiliar to readers of British industrial sociology. Hence, this theory emphasises cooperation, job satisfaction and members' contemporary characteristics such as skill level, age and family responsibilities; the ideological dimension of trade unionism is largely ignored and little or no attention is paid to a workers' past experiences, to the past events that have occurred in the workplace or, more importantly, to the development of national and worldwide labour movements and historical events, such as the 1930s' depression. I maintain that the 'stake-in-the-job' theory takes too narrow a view of trade unionism. It is also possible to participate because of a belief in the ideal of collectivism: the group pursuit of group goals. There is a certain amount of evidence available in the USA, as we shall see later, that shows trade union activism to be related to belief in group goals, to a concern with the political and social goals of trade unionism and to political attitudes and behaviour. But little attempt has been made to develop a theory of participation that includes an explanation of these findings and the 'stake-in-the-job' theorists have generally ignored them.

The argument that the 'stake-in-the-job' theory is unsatisfactory since it ignores both the historical and ideological aspects of trade unionism is even stronger when we try to apply this theory to participation in Great Britain or in other Western European countries where class consciousness is generally agreed to be greater and where the trade union movement's relationship with political parties has been so much closer. In the case of Great Britain in particular, there is a great deal of evidence, as we shall see in Chapter 6, which suggests that participation in trade unionism is more than a means whereby an individual defends his 'job interests'. The limited amount of empirical material available in British trade union literature also shows the specific contentions of the 'stake-in-the-job' theory not to be generally supported, although some support is offered to the contention that activity is correlated with being male rather than female[24] and, less strongly, with skill level[25] and seniority.[26] Thus the evidence on age[27] and attitude to management[28] is contradictory, that on marital status very limited,[29] and that on job satisfaction negative.[30] Not surprisingly, no one until now has investigated the relationship between activity and dual allegiance among British trade union members.

Other writers in the USA, in addition to the 'stake-in-the-job' theorists, have also taken up the idea that the actives are seeking in their participation certain individual ends which are essentially extrinsic to trade unionism.[31] These union members, similarly to those members with high job stakes, have positively evaluated local participation in terms of its 'costs' to their other roles (e.g. familial and leisure roles) as the most effective and efficient means to their ends. Thus Kyllonen (1951) stresses the extrinsic end of the need for social companionship since he maintains that those who attend meetings lack complete family-children-kin patterns. Specifically, Kyllonen (pp.530–2) maintains that in the local he studied, single union members were more active than married, the married but childless were more active than those married with children, and the more a union member visited with or was visited by relatives the less likely he was to be active. Gouldner (1957, p.389) sees the 'business unionist' as a well-known type of trade union leader, a leader who saw himself as the middle man involved in the sale of the union members' labour power to the employer and, as such, saw his office in entrepreneurial terms of pecuniary rewards, security and personal prestige. Sayles and Strauss (1967, pp.72–3) described a type of local leader – the 'administrative' leader – who saw his role in similar terms and coveted personal power, recognition and prestige. Similarly, Seidman *et al.* (1950, pp.233–4) found several local leaders referred to the satisfactory personal feelings their offices gave them.[32] On the whole, few of these theories sound very plausible and when their singular lack of empirical substantiation is considered the usefulness of them for a serious study of blue-collar union participation appears negligible.[33] The charge of ignoring the historical and ideological dimensions of trade unionism, which would be a particularly serious omission in any study of British participation, applies equally to this group of theories as it did to the 'stake-in-the-job' theory.[34]

It has also been suggested in the US literature on trade union participation that members seek local union positions in order to gain a full-time union job (see the description in Sayles and Strauss (1967, p.50) of their 'steward politician' and in Chinoy (1953, p.165) of his 'ambitious leader') or to be promoted within their firm to a foreman's position (Sayles and Strauss 1967, p.51).[35] Again, writers on this theme produce no quantitative material to support their claims; in any case, this would be a very difficult area in which to collect accurate information. But these suggestions, especially in the case of the desire for promotion to foreman, do sound more plausible than the previously discussed selective incentives that have been used to explain the occurrence of nonpathological participation in unionism.[36] However it is unlikely that they would be responsible for the motivation of more than a very small number of local/branch officials. There are, after all only a limited number of union posts or foreman's positions available. In addition, there are other forms of participation possible in the local or branch apart from that of holding office: the suggestions reviewed above would have little relevance for explaining local/branch or shop activities such as attending union meetings, reading the union journal or talking about union affairs with workmates.

Better documented in the USA has been the response of members of minority groups such as Negroes, Mexicans, Jews and Catholics to trade union participation as a means to combat colour, cultural and religious discrimination through the unions' emphasis on collective improvement and which has led to their higher levels of participation than those of the dominant ethnic group (Seidman *et al*. 1958, pp.193, 245; Form and Dansereau 1957, p.11; Purcell 1953A, pp.149, 154—5, 196; Shepard 1949, pp.313—5; Herberg 1953, pp.12—19). However, it is doubtful whether these studies provide any guidance for an investigation into blue-collar union participation in Great Britain, which has had a very different history of immigration and religious assimilation.[37]

In addition to these theories emphasising the extrinsic rewards of union participation on the group or individual level there are two further explanations of activism that have been suggested in the US literature. The first of these, the 'social activity' theory, explains participation in terms of personality factors, and the second, the 'technological determinism' theory, explains participation in terms of the operation of technological factors in the workplace.

The 'social activity' theory

This theory is most strongly put forward by Tannenbaum (1965), Tannenbaum and Kahn (1958), Kyllonen (1951) and Form and Dansereau (1957). The same theme has been suggested and significantly developed by Goldstein (1952) in the UK. According to this theory, the active unionist is a different kind of person from the inactive – more ascendent, outgoing and social, who seeks to derive satisfaction from doing things with people : thus he belongs to and takes an active part in other formal organisations, particularly those with a working class membership and social functions (Tannenbaum and Kahn 1958, pp. 88—90; Sayles and Strauss 1967, pp.71—2; Kyllonen 1951, p.532; Goldstein 1952, p.257). He also takes a greater part in informal social activity (Kyllonen 1951, p.532) and he has more friends both at work and in general (Tannenbaum and Kahn 1958, pp.78—80). At the same time, he has as many hobbies and interests as the inactive member and still manages to spend time with his family (Goldstein 1952, pp.258, 293). The most important characteristic of such actives is that they perceive the primary function of unionism to be that of 'providing a social world for its members' (Form and Dansereau 1957, pp.6—7). For these socially orientated actives, participation does not involve any 'costs' and is a source of reward of a kind not otherwise obtainable.

The empirical evidence available in the USA and the UK on the characteristics of active union members offers positive support to at least some of the contentions of the 'social activity' theory. Thus, while no one has actually administered personality tests to active and inactive local members, a number of union studies in the USA have noted the actives' possession of sociable personality traits (Seidman *et al*. 1958, pp.175, 191; Purcell 1953A, p.210; Sayles and Strauss 1952, pp.57—8, 74).[38] There is more substantial support in the US literature for the contention that active members have greater numbers of friends, both inside and outside the plant.[39] Also, although there is no substantive material available in the USA on the relationship between home life and union activity, Goldstein in the UK provides convincing proof

9

that active members have equally broad, if not broader, scope of hobbies, interests and spare time activities as do inactive members and, in addition, 'help around the house' as frequently.[40] However, as regards the 'social activity' theorists' proposals for the 'active members' views on union goals, the empirical evidence is distinctly lacking[41] and, as regards the actives' participation in other voluntary associations, is contradictory.[42] Further, there is little information available on the actives' level of informal social activity.[43] It should also be pointed out here that this theory relies too heavily on the distribution of individual personality traits: in accounting for the phenomenon of trade union participation, sociological factors would surely be expected to play at least some part. This theory is worth considering, nevertheless, as a minor explanatory theme, to be combined with some broader and more sociological theory of participation.[44]

The 'technological implications' approach

The importance of the influence of technology has frequently been stressed in the explanation of industrial behaviour and the phenomenon of trade union participation is no exception.[45] According to this theory, again most frequently put forward in the USA, attitudes and behaviour at work, including attitudes towards unionism and participation in the branch, are primarily determined by the type of productive technology in operation: more specifically, by the way in which the work tasks and work roles are defined and by the way in which these tasks and roles are related to each other and coordinated.

Thus Sayles and Strauss (1967, pp.83–4) and Seidman *et al*. (1958, pp.132–3) assert that job accessibility (the extent of movement and contact allowed by or involved in a worker's job) plays an important part in participation. Sayles and Strauss (pp.114–7) go on to assert that work groups whose members are homogeneous in skill, pay, work tasks and background are more likely to participate than heterogeneous groups. Tannenbaum and Kahn (1958, pp.100–3) argue that, since the union is organised and orientated around the job and the member's stake in his job appears to be the important determinant of his union activity, the 'time-space' dimensions – the physical location – of that worker's differentially-valued job have significant effects in turn on his thinking and behaviour in relation to the union. However the only serious empirical investigation into the correlation of the workplace and activity is, in fact, their own study and their evidence partly proves and partly disproves the contentions of this theory.[46]

The 'technological implications' theory of union activity, as well as lacking convincing empirical substantiation, can also be seriously criticised on theoretical grounds. In fact, the whole 'technological implications' approach to industrial sociology has been widely criticised, especially in recent years, and it is only necessary to show briefly how the general criticisms made of this approach can be applied to technologically-orientated explanations of trade union participation.[47] Thus the 'technological implications' approach as applied to union activism neglects: (1) influence on workers' attitudes and behaviour of their own definition of the work situation, which may to some extent be independent of the objective technological features; (2) the roles played by the union members in out-of-work contexts as members of such groups as families, communities, political parties, pressure groups and social classes, which can considerably influence their attitudes and behaviour at work; and

(3) any consideration of historical factors, including the individual's past experience at work and in the community, the workplace's previous industrial relations record and more widely experienced events such as the 1926 General Strike.

In order to investigate the characteristics and motivation of blue-collar branch actives, I did not want to look at an industrial situation that was part of one of those traditional industries such as mining, docking and shipbuilding which, together with their isolated and solidary communities, are, to an ever-increasing extent, backwaters of national, industrial and urban development (Lockwood 1966, pp.254–5). Nor, on the other hand, did I want a prototypical industrial situation characterised by highly instrumentally orientated and mobile workers as was the case in 'The Affluent Worker' study. Instead I preferred a situation that was part of a viable industry and which could yield a model of blue-collar branch activism which had possibilities of application to a wide range of industrial situations. Other important considerations were: that the union branches should be shop-based, as this would cut down variation in respondents' work situations; that the union should have a closed-shop policy, so that all extremes of inactivity should be included in the membership; and that to avoid the further complication of sexual role differences, the workers should all be male.

With these considerations in mind, a steel plant in the then-profitable Special Steels Division of British Steel Corporation was chosen. This was a large plant situated in the Sheffield/Rotherham conurbation: an area whose economy is heavily dependent on steel-making and associated industries. The plant covered just over 200 acres of a 500 acre site and it was ESC's boast when it commenced production ·in 1963 that it was 'Europe's most modern steel plant'.[48] The steelworkers in this plant belonged to the British Iron and Steel and Kindred Trades Association.[49]

To get a reasonable number of active members to provide a sound basis for statistical analysis, it was necessary to combine the actives from two branches. One particular advantage of the steel plant chosen was that it contained three separate shops, two of which were sited fairly close together, were roughly of the same size and had been built at the same time. It was decided to use the two BISAKTA branches based on these two shops for the survey: these were the Melting Shop branch and the Bloom and Billet Mill branch.

11

2

THE PARTICIPATION SURVEY

The first step in any serious study of branch participation is to identify the actives.[1] As we saw in Chapter 1, several definitions of activity have been used; however, apart from Lipset *et al.* (1956, pp.437–8) and Tannenbaum and Kahn (1958, Chapter 4), who constructed indices, writers in this field have tended to concentrate on one aspect of participation, usually either attendance at branch/local meetings or holding branch/local office. These authors' definitions can also be criticised on the grounds that, with the exceptions of Beynon (1973) and Lane and Roberts (1971), they have concentrated exclusively on formal participation and neglected informal and shop participation.[2] It has been argued in the USA by Kovner and Lahne (1953) and by Seidman *et al.* (1958) and, in Great Britain, by Roberts (1956, pp. 57–69, 111–12), Cyriax and Oakeshott (1960, pp.67–8) and, more recently, by McCarthy and Parker (1968) that shop or workplace unionism is at least as important as, if not more so than, branch unionism.

In this study's definition and measurement of activism, as many aspects of participation as possible were included and informal and shop as well as formal branch participation were emphasised. To solve the problem of identifying the actives, it was decided to conduct a preliminary participation survey of members in the Melting Shop branch and the Bloom and Billet Mill branch. A self-completed, pre-coded questionnaire was designed that covered twelve different aspects of participation, six formal and six informal or shop-orientated, and was administered to all members of the two branches.

The description of the contents of this questionnaire begins by looking at the questions on the formal aspects of participation.[3] The first of these is attendance at branch meetings, which were held in the case of both branches once a month on Sunday mornings in the backrooms of pubs.[4] The respondents were asked here how frequently they attended these meetings and also, as a check question, whether or not they had attended the last branch meeting.[5] The respondents were also asked if they went to branch meetings 'sometimes' or more frequently, how much they talked at them. Secondly, the respondents were asked how frequently they voted in elections for union officials, which took place once a year at the branch meeting. They were also asked, as a check question, whether they had voted in the last election for union officials.[6]

Thirdly, the respondents were asked whether they had asked the branch to take up any grievances on their behalf during the previous year and, if so, how many. Fourthly, the respondents were asked if they had attended any educational courses on trade unionism and, if so, to indicate which on the list printed on the questionnaire.[7] Finally, the respondents were asked a series of questions concerning both their membership of union committees and their holding of union offices.[8] They were asked if they were on any union committees that year, and, if so, to tick the appropriate committee or committees in the list printed on the questionnaire. They were then asked if they had been on any union committees before that year and again given a list of committees. The same procedure was followed for the holding of union positions for that year and for previous years.[9]

Turning to the question on informal or shop participation, the respondents were asked first of all how frequently they attended the shop meetings held when necessary on the site. The respondents were then asked, as a check question, in the case of the Melting Shop whether or not they had attended the shop meeting held on March 1971 to discuss the redundancy issue or, in the case of the Bloom and Billet Mill, how many out of the four shop meetings held in August 1970 to discuss the new tonnage bonus they had attended. The respondents were also asked if they went to shop meetings 'sometimes' or more frequently, how much they talked at them. Secondly, the respondents were asked how familiar they were with the contents of the BISAKTA rulebook and given a choice of answers, including the answer 'I didn't know there was a rulebook'. Thirdly, the respondents were asked how frequently they read the BISAKTA journal *Man and Metal* and were again given a choice of answers, similarly including the answer 'I have never heard of *Man and Metal*'. If the respondents read this journal 'sometimes' or more frequently, they were asked, as a check question, how much of it they read and were given a choice of answers including the answer 'I only really glance at the cover'. Fourthly, the respondents were asked how frequently they talked to their workmates about union affairs either at work or away from work and were also asked, as a check question, when they had last in fact done so. Fifthly, the respondents were asked how frequently they talked to their branch officials or committeemen about their work and conditions and again, as a check question, when they had last done so. Finally, the respondents were asked how much they helped canvass in the annual elections for the Executive Council members and were given a choice of answers including the answer 'I didn't know there were any elections for Executive Council members'. They were also asked, as a check question, if they had helped in the Executive Council elections in 1969 in the case of the Bloom and Billet Mill, or the 1970 election in the case of the Melting Shop.

In addition, the respondents were asked for details of their department, job, rota, date and place of birth and length of time they had been employed at the steelworks. The purpose of these questions was (1) to eliminate certain categories of respondents and (2) to compare, as far as possible, the social characteristics of the respondents with those of the non-respondents.[10]

Table A1.1 in Appendix 1 gives a summary of the participation questionnaire findings for the two branches and there are some general points to be made here before we go on to discuss the respondents' overall scores. First of all, the general level of participation appears to be much the same for the two branches, although the pattern of participation appears to differ slightly.[11] The members of the Melting Shop branch placed a greater stress on the more formal aspects of attending branch meetings and voting in union elections, while the members of the Bloom and Billet Mill branch placed more stress on talking to their workmates about union affairs.

This suggests that those interested in union affairs in the Melting Shop tended to go to the branch meetings to find out what was happening, while in the Bloom and Billet Mill the smaller number of members who did attend the branch meeting tended to act as sources of information for all those interested in union affairs. The participation pattern of the members of both branches, however, equally emphasised the shop meetings.

Secondly, there was a good correspondence between the respondents' answers to the questions where they rated their own level of participation and their answers to the factual questions. For example, 64 of the respondents in the Melting Shop and 41 of the respondents in the Bloom and Billet Mill claimed to vote 'regularly' or 'fairly regularly' in elections for union officers and this claim is validated by the fact that 62 of the former and 36 of the latter actually voted in the last such election.

Finally, the level of formal participation in the two branches appears to be fairly typical for union branches in Great Britain. The proportion in the Bloom and Billet Mill branch who had attended the last branch meeting, 19 per cent, compares well with Roberts' (1956, pp.95–7) estimate that among workers in long-established heavy industry and craft workers, rates of attendance at meetings were similar to those of the woodworkers who averaged between 15 and 20 per cent, and with the maximum attendance figures of 15–20 per cent (calculated on the basis of voting figures) reported by Political and Economic Planning (1948, pp.25–6) for 16 larger-than-average unions. It also compares well with *The Dockworker's* (p.122) finding that 20 per cent of those interviewed claimed to have attended one or more branch meetings in four. (However, the proportion who had attended the last meeting in the Melting Shop at 31 per cent seems to be a little higher.[12])

Full details of the scoring system are given in Appendix 1. This was based on the respondents' replies to the questions where they were required to rate their own level of participation together with their use of the branch's grievance procedure, their attendance at courses on trade unionism and their holding of any union office or position. In devising this system an attempt was made to balance as far as possible the formal and informal aspects of participation and to include some reference to the respondents' previous history of participation.

The respondents' overall scores are summarised by the histogram in Figure 2.1.[13] Here we can see that the distribution of the respondents' scores approximated very roughly to a positive skewed normal curve with the majority of the scores ranging from 0 to 35. The actives have been defined by cutting off the positive 'tail' of the distribution between the 12th and 13th scores. The actual cut-off point was to some extent arbitrary but there was a suggestive 'break' in the shape of the histogram at this point and the number of actives this gave accorded well with pragmatic and statistical considerations. It was also felt to be essential to select for study an inactive 'control' group with which to compare the actives. Thus it was decided to cut off the negative 'tail' of the distribution for this purpose. It would also have been possible to select such a control group by conducting a random sample of all those respondents not included in the active group. However, it was felt that by using the most inactive respondents, the sharpest contrast with the active respondents could be obtained in what was essentially an explorative study of branch participation and thus make the most efficient use of scarce resources. The actual cut-off point, between the 5th and 6th scores, was again to some extent arbitrary but there was another suggestive

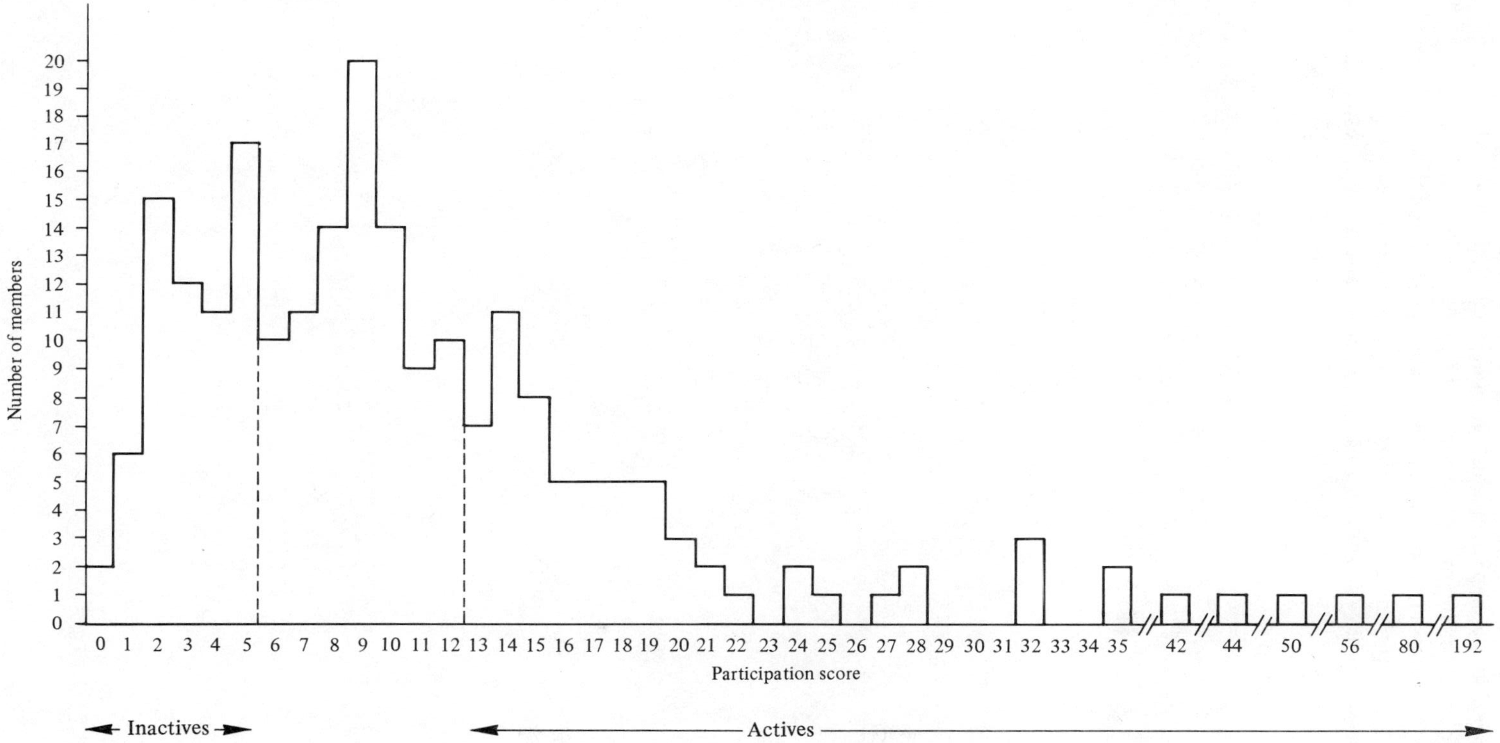

Figure 2.1   Distribution of participation scores for the Melting Shop and Bloom and Billet Mill combined

'break' in the shape of the histogram here and, in addition, this gave approximately the same number of inactives as actives.

Thus the definition of an active branch member in this study was a participation score of 13 or more and the definition of an inactive one was a score of 5 or less. These definitions yielded a total of 68 actives and 63 inactives for the main interview survey.[14]

3

TESTING THE US THEORIES OF LOCAL ACTIVISM IN A BRITISH CONTEXT

In the previous chapter I described the method used to identify and select the in-active and active respondents in the Melting Shop and Bloom and Billet Mill of the BSC steelworks with which this study of blue-collar trade union participation is concerned. In this chapter I will consider the survey findings on the factors central to the 'political agitator', to the 'stake-in-the-job' and other theories stressing the extrinsic ends of trade unionism, to the 'social activity' theory and to the 'techno-logical implications' approach as outlined in Chapter 1. Specifically, I will examine the more factual aspects of these sets of theories; the more complicated and less tangible question of the steelworkers' perception of the purpose of trade unions will be examined in the next chapter.[1]

Survey findings relevant to theories of local activism stressing extrinsic ends
This section begins with the more factual aspects of the 'stake-in-the-job' theory as this, as we have seen, has been the most consistently put forward to ex-plain local participation, particularly in the USA. The questions the survey needed to answer here were 'Did the actives possess, to a greater extent than their inactive counterparts, those characteristics which would lead them to place a higher premium on their jobs?' and 'Were the actives distinguished from the inactives by their higher level of job satisfaction and more cooperative attitude towards management?'.

Dealing first with the question of possession of the specified social characteristics, it was found (and indeed this was perhaps the most significant finding of the entire survey for historical reasons as well as in the interests of testing the 'stake-in-the-job' theory) that the active respondents were not significantly older than the inactive. The distributions of the dates of birth for both groups were very similar: the median age for the actives was 45 years and that for the inactives 38 years, while the age ranges for the two groups were 22 to 62 in both cases. However, age does play a crucial role in the analysis of the survey findings, as we shall see, since there were important differences in the characteristics of the younger (those less than 40 years old at the time of the interview) and older (those aged 40 years or more) actives as compared to their inactive counterparts.[2]

However, the active and inactive respondents did differ significantly with regard to skill and seniority levels. Dealing with the question of skill first, use was made of each steel worker's 'job percentage bonus rating', which was based on the skill re-quired by that job and which played a large part in determining the size of the worker's pay packet. This bonus rating provided an easily determined and usefully combined measure of the respondent's wage and skill levels and avoided asking the

Table 3.1   *Respondents' Job Percentage Bonus Ratings*

Bonus rating	Inactive	Active
%	%	%
45–55	66.1	37.9
56–65	20.3	30.3
66–75	11.9	18.2
76–85	0	6.1
86–100	1.7	7.6
Total	100	100
	(N=59)	(N=66)

Note: 1-tailed K–S test, P = 0.005, G = 0.48.

respondent for details of his wage packet, which might have reduced the respondents' cooperation in the interview. Table 3.1 gives the job percentage bonus ratings for the two groups and shows clearly that the actives had significantly higher ratings than the inactives: nearly a third of the actives were in the top three categories compared to only 14 per cent of the inactives. The degree of association here was moderately high in relation to the scores obtained in the survey in general.

Table 3.2 shows the relationship between seniority and activity. Here, well over three-quarters of the actives compared to about half of the inactives had been employed at the steel works for seven or eight years (i.e. since the steelworks was first opened). This difference was significant and the degree of association between seniority and activity was higher than in the previous case of skill and activity. However, when age was controlled for, important differences were found between the younger and older respondents. The degree of association between seniority and activity remained roughly the same for the younger respondents, whereas the relationship between the two variables was not significant for the older ones. This difference between the two age groups was due to the younger actives, in common with both the older actives and inactives, tending to have joined the steelworks as soon as it was opened whereas the younger inactives tended to have joined a year or so later. Consequently, the proportions of younger and older actives in the highest seniority category in the table were fairly similar.

Turning to the last of the specified social characteristics of the active – his greater tendency to marry – Table A3.1 shows that the actives were indeed significantly more likely to be currently married than the inactives: 24 per cent of the inactives were single, separated, divorced or widowed compared to only 4 per cent of the actives. The degree of association between being currently married and activity was moderate at 0.41. It can reasonably also be argued (although none of the proponents of the 'stake-in-the-job' theory has done so) that activity will vary according to the number of children a worker has who are financially dependent on him. To test this contention, it was calculated for each respondent who was, or had been, married, the number of children he had who were either aged under 14 years or were over 14 but still at school. Here no difference was found initially between the active and inactive respondents in numbers of dependent children. But when age was controlled

Table 3.2   *Number of years respondents employed at steelworks*

Number of years	(i) All		(ii) Under 40 years		(iii) 40 years and over	
	Inactive %	Active %	Inactive %	Active %	Inactive %	Active %
1 – 2	11.9	4.5	9.7	4.0	14.3	4.8
3 – 4	15.3	4.5	19.4	8.3	10.7	2.4
5 – 6	23.7	7.6	38.7	12.5	7.1	4.8
7 – 8	49.2	83.3	32.3	75.0	67.9	88.1
Total	100	100	100	100	100	100
	(*N*=59)	(*N*=66)	(*N*=31)	(*N*=24)	(*N*=28)	(*N*=42)

Notes: Column (i)   1-tailed K–S test P = 0.001, G = 0.61.
 Column (ii)   1-tailed K–S test P = 0.01, G = 0.60.
 Column (iii) 1-tailed K–S test P $>$ 0.10.

for, it was found that the younger actives did have a significantly greater number of dependent children, as can be seen from columns (ii) and (iii) of Table A3.2; in fact just over a half of the younger actives had three or more dependent children compared to under a quarter of their inactive counterparts. The degree of association here was moderately high at 0.47. Column (iii) of this table shows that there continued to be no relationship between number of dependent children and activity for the older respondents. It appears that the younger active steelworkers got married and started their families earlier than their inactive counterparts.

Summarising the survey's findings so far, it appears that there is no support for the 'stake-in-the-job' theorists' contention that actives are older than inactive members. But there was support for the contentions that they are more highly skilled and more likely to be married. However, support for the contention that actives had higher job seniority than inactive members and the contention, logically deriving from these theorists' views on marital status, that actives had more dependent children, held only in the case of the younger branch members.

The second general question that needs to be asked in this study of steelworks concerned the actives' greater levels of both job satisfaction and cooperativeness towards management. Both of these indicators of job stake required careful operationalisation. In particular, job satisfaction needs to be measured in a more meaningful and methodologically sophisticated way than the proponents of the 'stake-in-the-job' theory have so far attempted.

The first step in analysing the steelworkers' levels of job satisfaction is, as was discussed in Chapter 1, to establish what aspects of their jobs were most important to them. The respondents' expectations of selected aspects of their jobs were all measured in the same way. The respondent was told that there were a number of things often thought important about a job and that the interviewer was interested in finding out how important the various aspects of a job were to the respondent personally. He was then asked to rate the importance of each of the selected aspects by placing an X on a scale of importance printed on the interview schedule. These scales ranged from 0 to 100 and were marked off at five-point intervals, with every 25th point having a descriptive label.[3]

Table 3.3   *Respondents' Levels of Expectation and Satisfaction for Selected Aspects of their Job Situation.*

Aspect of job situation	(i) Aspect importance-median rating		(ii) Aspect satisfaction-median rating		(iii) Level of significance for differences in satisfaction found between active and inactive respondents	(iv) Degree of association (G) between activity and a higher level of job satisfaction
	Inactive (N=59)	Active (N=66)	Inactive (N=59)	Active (N=66)		
Job security	100	100	65	75	0.05	0.37
Strong and active union branch	95	100	75	75	0.05	0.39
Friendly, sociable and pleasant workmates	95	95	80	95	> 0.10	–
Very high wages	85	95	75	75	> 0.10	–
Getting along well with shift foreman	90	85	75	90	0.05	0.26

Notes: Column (i)   The importance median ratings for the other five selected job aspects were: interest and variety, inactives 75%, actives 85%; opportunity to use skill, inactives 75%, actives 80%; opportunity to use initiative and take responsibility, inactives 75%, actives 85%; being able to talk to other people while working, inactives 50%, actives 50%; management's taking an interest in respondent, inactives 75%, actives 75%.

Column (iii) Calculated using a one-tailed K – S test.

Column (iv) The respondents' ratings were grouped into five categories for the calculation of the degree of association here: 0 to 12.5, 12.5 to 37.5, 37.5 to 62.5, 62.5 to 87.5 and 87.5 to 100.

Column (i) (with its accompanying footnote) of Table 3.3 gives the median scores of the actives' and inactives' assessment of importance of each of the work aspects included in the survey and shows that in general both groups had high levels of expectation of their work. They were most of all concerned with job security but they also rated as being very important agreeable workmates, very high wages, a good relationship with the foreman and a forceful union branch; for these aspects, the median ratings ranged from 85 to 100 per cent. Of slightly less importance to the respondents (the median ratings ranged from 65 to 85 per cent) were opportunities to exercise initiative and use skill, having interest and variety in their work and feeling that management took an interest in them on the personal level. The respondents considered talking scope while working to be of limited importance. For the five work aspects considered by the steelworkers as a whole to be the most important, the active and inactives' ratings were compared and in only one aspect – that of having a strong and active union branch – was there any difference between the two groups and this in statistical terms was only a suggestive and not a significant difference.[4] The active and inactive respondents' views on the importance of job security, pleasant workmates, high wages and having a good foreman relationship were very similar.[5]

The steelworkers' levels of job satisfaction were measured in a very similar manner to that in which their levels of job expectation were measured.[6] For each of the aspects of their jobs for which they had previously been asked to assess the importance, they were asked to state their level of satisfaction with it by placing an X on a scale of satisfaction printed on the interview schedule, this scale closely resembling in construction that used in measuring job expectations.[7] The median scores for the active and inactive groups' ratings of their satisfaction with what they considered to be the five most important aspects of their jobs are given in column (ii) of Table 3.3. The median ratings given in the column in fact show both groups to be reasonably satisfied with these aspects of their jobs – the median ratings ranging from 65 to 90 per cent – but they obviously felt there was room for improvement.[8] The active and inactive members' satisfaction ratings for these five job aspects were compared and, as column (iii) of Table 3.3 shows, the actives' levels of satisfaction were significantly higher than those of the inactives in the case of job security, branch performance and relationship with foreman.[9] However, as column (iv) of the same table shows, the degrees of association in these cases were moderate to low, being particularly low in the case of getting along well with the foreman. In addition, we should note that the job aspect where there was the highest association between activity and a high level of satisfaction was that of estimate of branch performance and this finding can perhaps more convincingly be explained in terms of the actives' greater involvement in their branch rather than as an indication of their being 'solid citizens'.[10] Again, the association between greater satisfaction with job security and activity could be alternatively interpreted as simply reflecting the actives' higher levels of seniority, particularly in the case of the younger actives.

Certain of the 'stake-in-the-job' theorists, as we have seen, used numbers of work-friends as a particular measure of job satisfaction and we are consequently obliged to examine the survey findings in this respect. The steelworkers were asked how many of the people they worked with they would consider to be 'close friends'.[11] Column (i) of Table A3.3 gives the results of this question and shows that the active group were, in fact, suggestively more likely to consider at least one of the people they worked with as a close friend: over half of the actives (56 per cent) did so compared to 39 per cent of the inactives. The degree of association here was low, however, at 0.24. In contrast, the survey results corresponding to the slightly different measure used by Dean do not support even to a limited extent, the 'stake-in-the-job' theory's contention.[12] Thus column (ii) of the same table shows that, although the great majority of both active and inactive respondents in the survey did carry their work relationships over into their out-of-work lives, the inactives rather than the actives were a little more likely to do so. This means that although the actives were suggestively more likely than the inactives to have close friends at work, they were not significantly or suggestively more likely to see someone they worked with outside of work: between a third and a half of both groups (47 per cent and 37 per cent respectively) saw one or more of the people they worked with outside of work on a regular basis. We should also note here that the previous significant finding on the greater number of friends at work possessed by the active group is capable of alternative explanation: that it is a reflection of a greater sociability drive on the part of the actives. The plausibility of this interpretation is supported, as we shall see later, by the survey findings that the actives also displayed greater sociability in the contexts of participation in voluntary associations and informal social activity.

Summarising the survey's findings on the steelworkers' levels of job satisfaction, it emerged first of all, that while the active members did experience a sense of job satisfaction, their overall level of job satisfaction was not as high as that suggested by the 'stake-in-the-job' theorists. Secondly, it emerged that the active members' levels of job satisfaction were not clearly higher than those of the inactive members: although the actives experienced significantly higher satisfaction for three out of the five job aspects, the degrees of association were low and two out of the three positive relationships could in fact reflect other factors. The positive finding for number of friends and activity is again a moderate one in terms of degree of association and also permits alternative explanation.

The measurement of attitude towards management needs, as stated previously, the same care as that of job satisfaction. The survey attempted to measure the branch members' attitude towards management by looking at: how in their opinion, BSC's management compared with that of other firms in the area; their attitude to promotion both of themselves and branch officials; and, finally, their attitude towards taking up grievances. The specific purpose was to test the 'stake-in-the-job' theorists' contention that the active had a more favourable opinion of and was more cooperative towards, management.

The survey revealed that both the active and inactive groups felt BSC's management compared moderately favourably with that of other firms in the Sheffield/Rotherham area: 31 out of 66 actives (47 per cent) and 23 out of 59 inactives (39 per cent) considered their management to be 'about average' and a further 14 actives (21 per cent) and 11 inactives (19 per cent) chose 'quite a bit better'. Hardly any respondents (three actives and two inactives) considered their management any worse than average and only 10 actives (15 per cent) and 17 inactives (29 per cent) considered it 'very much better'.[13]

The steelworkers were also asked in an open-ended question why they felt the way they did about BSC's management. An analysis of their replies here shows that the most frequently given reason by both active and inactive groups for having a favourable opinion of management to at least some extent – given by 16 out of 47 actives (34 per cent) and 16 out of 42 inactives (38 per cent) – was that there was a good relationship between men and management at BSC: the management were thought to be 'fair' and 'reasonable'. The second most frequently given reason – given by 15 actives (32 per cent) and 8 inactives (19 per cent) – was that there were good conditions and amenities at BSC: the respondents felt that the management tried to 'do a lot' for the workers.[14]

The respondents were further asked how far they agreed or disagreed with the statement 'BSC could afford to pay higher wages than it does now without damaging its prospects for the future'. Here it was found that, despite their moderately favourable opinion of management, both groups generally agreed with this statement: 40 out of 66 actives (61 per cent) either 'strongly agreed' or 'mildly agreed' and so did 32 out of 59 inactives (54 per cent).

Although the active and inactive respondents had generally favourable attitudes towards management, neither of the two groups wished to become members of management themselves; they preferred to remain on the shop floor. Thus, when the respondents were asked how much they would like to become a shift foreman, 52 out of 66 actives (79 per cent) and 48 out of 59 inactives (81 per cent) chose the replies 'not at all' or 'not very much'.[15] Both groups (16 out of 52 actives (31 per cent) and 19 out of 48 inactives (40 per cent)) primarily stressed specific features of a shift foreman's job that they disliked such as 'too much responsibility', being 'piggy-in-the-middle' or 'too much hanging around'.[16]

In answering the question of how they would feel if a branch official accepted promotion to a management position, the majority of both the active and inactive groups chose the reply 'no feelings either way' (44 out of 66 actives (67 per cent) and 33 out of 57 inactives (56 per cent)). Only a third or less of the two groups (16 (24 per cent) actives and 19 (32 per cent) inactives) chose 'mildly disapprove' or 'strongly disapprove'.[17] The respondents were again asked why they had chosen their particular replies and here nearly all the respondents with 'no feelings either way' said either that 'it's a man's own business' or that it was a matter of no importance to the union.[18] Nearly all of the minority who disapproved to some degree, whether they were active or inactive, had ideological objections to a branch official becoming a shift foreman.[19]

Up to now the survey findings on the active and inactive respondents' attitudes towards management have suggested that their feelings were fairly benign: both groups had moderately favourable opinions of their management based on a positive evaluation both of the prevailing relationship between men and management at their steelworks and of the provision by management of agreeable conditions and amenities. Although they preferred to remain on the shop floor themselves, this view was conditioned mainly by what were regarded as unpleasant features of the shift foreman's job, and in addition, they were largely indifferent as to whether a branch official accepted promotion or not. Only a small minority of respondents had ideological objections to themselves or a branch official becoming one of management thereby suggesting that they saw a cleavage between union and management; and not only was this proportion small – less than a third of each group in all

Table 3.4	Propensity to take up job grievances with union for respondents with experience of one or more	
	Inactive	Active
	%	%
Always take it up	16.7	42.9
Usually take it up	29.2	38.8
Sometimes take it up, sometimes let it go by	33.3	16.3
Usually let it go by	20.8	2.0
Always let it go by	0	0
Total	100	100
	(N=24)	(N=49)

Note: K − S test, P = 0.05, G = 0.59.

cases – but its adherents were equally drawn from the active and inactive groups. However, the final item in the discussion of attitudes towards management, that of the respondents' propensity to take up grievances through union channels, revealed important differences between the two groups: the actives were in fact far more aggressive here towards management than the inactives.

The respondents were first of all asked a filter question: whether they had ever had a job grievance of any sort. Those who had had experience of one or more job grievances were then asked how frequently they took up these grievances with the union.[20] Table 3.4 summarises their response to this question. Here we can see that the actives were much more likely to take their grievances up: the great majority of the actives chose the replies 'always' or 'usually take it up' compared to under half of the inactives. The degree of association here between propensity to take up grievances and activity was moderately high.[21]

The considerable discrepancy shown in the survey results between the actives' attitude towards taking up grievances and their response to the other questions on attitudes towards management, suggests that the question on grievances has not in fact tapped the actives' basic orientation to management. Instead, since the actives' response to this question (as we shall see later) closely resembled that obtained when the actives' attitudes towards striking were investigated, it is reasonable to suggest that what has been tapped is the actives' basic orientation towards trade unionism, of which attitude towards taking up grievances is an important part.[22] Thus if the findings for this final item in the investigation of the active and inactive respondents' attitudes towards management are disregarded, on the grounds that it should properly be considered as part of the respondents' trade union orientation, the previous conclusion that the actives and inactives both had moderately favourable attitudes towards management still stands. This conclusion does not support the contention of the 'stake-in-the-job' theorists that the active has a much more highly favourable opinion of the management than the inactive member.

Having progressed this far in the analysis of the survey results, we are now in a position to examine the survey findings for the active's possession of the composite characteristics of 'dual allegiance' and 'social integration'. Both of these composite variables, it will be remembered, were considered by various proponents of the 'stake-in-the-job' theory to be importantly linked to participation in union locals. In the case of dual allegiance, it was proposed that the active had a highly favourable attitude to *both* the union local and management, while the inactive member had a favourable attitude to only one of these or neither, and, in the case of social integration, it was proposed that the active simultaneously experienced greater job satisfaction, had a higher seniority rating and saw more of his workmates outside the plant than did the inactive member.

To measure 'dual allegiance', the respondents' replies to the survey question on how they felt BSC's management compared to that of other firms was combined with their rating of their satisfaction with the job their BISAKTA branch was doing in looking after the branch members' interests.[23] These two variables were then cross-tabulated, controlling for activity, and it was found that only a small proportion of the actives had highly favourable attitudes towards both management and branch, and that, in addition, there was no difference between the numbers of actives and inactives who did so: 23 out of 66 actives (35 per cent) possessed 'dual allegiance' as did 18 out of 59 inactives (30 per cent).

To measure 'social integration', it was first of all necessary to create a new variable, to correspond to Dean's 'satisfaction with work tasks performed', which consisted of the arithmetic average of the respondents' ratings of their satisfaction with the 'interest and variety', 'opportunity to use skill', and 'opportunity to use initiative and take responsibility' offered by their jobs. This new variable was then combined with the survey's findings on the number of workmates the respondents saw outside of work and the respondents' seniority ratings.[24] The higher category for each of these three variables was then scored as 1 and the lower as 0 and an index of social integration was generated, which was then cross-tabulated with activity. Here it was found that only 11 out of the 66 actives (17 per cent) in fact had a score of 3, i.e. they satisfied all the requirements of the social integration variable: they had a high degree of satisfaction with their work tasks, saw their workmates outside of work and had a high seniority rating.[25] Thus it can be concluded that there was little evidence to support the specific contention of the 'stake-in-the-job' theory that the actives, in contrast to the inactives, possessed the characteristic of 'dual allegiance' or were more socially integrated.

When this discussion of the survey's findings concerning the more factual aspects of the 'stake-in-the-job' theory commenced, two questions were asked: the first of these was whether the actives possessed to a greater degree than the inactives those characteristics which would lead them to place a high premium on their job. The survey findings did show this to be so for the important skill factor for both older and younger respondents. However with respect to the equally, if not more, important age factor, there was no difference between the active and inactive groups and, with respect to the again important seniority factor, the relationship only held for the younger members. Marital status and number of dependent children are perhaps slightly less important factors in the 'stake-in-the-job' theory, but the survey findings here were similar to those described above: thus while the marital status relationship was upheld for both older and younger respondents, the number of dependent children relationship only held for the younger ones.

The second question asked at the beginning of this discussion was whether the actives distinguished themselves from the inactives by their high level of job satisfaction and their highly favourable opinions of and cooperative attitude towards management. In the event, both groups experienced modest levels of job satisfaction and had moderately favourable attitudes towards management. Finally, in the case of the two composite variables, the survey produced no evidence indicating that the actives, in contrast to the inactives, possessed 'dual allegiance' or that the actives were more socially integrated than the inactives. A further important point that needs to be made here is that the relationship between skill level and activity – perhaps the best demonstrated incidence of support in this section for the 'stake-in-the-job' theory – can be interpreted, and very plausibly so, in a different manner as we shall see later.

With regard to other theories of local activism stressing the role of extrinsic individual ends, it would appear that the value of most of these cannot be properly assessed in this chapter, as they are mainly concerned with the actives' motivational patterns, the survey findings for which will be examined in the next chapter. In fact, it is possible in this chapter to discuss the survey findings only in relation to Kyllonen's contentions on the active and inactive members' family-children-kin patterns. We have already seen in the previous discussion of the survey findings in relation to the 'stake-in-the-job' theory, that those who attended local meetings were, contrary to Kyllonen's contention, less rather than more likely to be single. In addition, column (i) of Table A3.2 shows actives to have had a significantly greater number of children in total than had the inactive members, contrary to Kyllonen's assertion that those who were married but childless would be more active than those married and with children. Indeed the degree of association between activity and having a larger number of children in total was 0.31[26]. The survey of Sheffield steelworkers did not provide any specific data on amount of kin visiting, as Kyllonen did. But the survey did yield the information that active and inactive respondents tended to have the same number of living kin, the median number for both groups being 10 kin members.[27] This information, added to the previous findings on marital status and number of children, very strongly suggests that activists did *not* lack a complete kin pattern as Kyllonen suggests they do.

With regard to the last theory of local activism to be considered in this section, that of the 'political agitator' which stresses the role of group extrinsic ends, the only survey finding relevant here is the steelworkers' membership or non-membership of extreme left-wing political parties. In fact none of the actives nor inactives belonged to such parties.[28]

Survey findings relevant to the 'social activity' theory

The questions the survey needed to answer here were 'Were the active members more outgoing, ascendent and social than the inactive ones?' and 'Did the actives, accordingly, take a greater part in social activities both of a formal and an informal kind than did the inactives, and were the actives likely to have more social acquaintances?'.

We will begin by looking at the steelworkers' participation in formal social activities, specifically in voluntary associations other than trade unions. The respondents were asked if they belonged to any clubs, societies or organisations: for example, a sports club, a church, a political party, a workingman's club or a BSC club. They were then asked how often they attended social affairs of the voluntary associations they

Table 3.5   *Respondents' membership of and participation in non-union voluntary associations*

Number of voluntary associations	(i) Membership		(ii) Participation (for members only)	
	Inactive %	Active %	Inactive %	Active %
0	10.2	7.6	28.3	8.2
1	45.8	21.2	60.4	55.7
2	32.2	42.4	9.4	24.6
3	10.2	21.2	1.9	9.8
4 or more	1.7	7.6	0	1.6
Total	100 (N=59)	100 (N=66)	100 (N=53)	100 (N=61)

Notes: Column (i) 1-tailed K–S test $P = 0.01$, $G = 0.41$.
Column (ii)1-tailed K–S test $P = 0.05$, $G = 0.59$.

belonged to in relation to how frequently meetings etc., were held. They were also asked if they held an official position or were on any committee in any of the voluntary associations they belonged to.

Column (i) of Table 3.5 gives details of the number of non-union voluntary associations the respondents belonged to. Here we can see that the active respondents belonged to a significantly greater number than the inactives: the median number belonged to by the actives was two and that of the inactives one. The degree of association here between belonging to other formal associations and union activity was moderate.[29]

But more important for our purposes here is to find out how many voluntary associations the respondents took an *active* part in: that is active in relation to the maximum amount of participation that was possible in each voluntary association. Column (ii) of Table 3.5 shows that, taking voluntary association members only, the actives participated in a significantly greater number of non-union voluntary associations than the inactives did. Although the median number participated in was one for both groups, over a third of the actives participated in more than one compared to just over 10 per cent of the inactives. The degree of association here between voluntary association participation and union activity was higher than in the case of membership. In addition, 11 out of 61 actives (18 per cent) compared to only 2 out of 53 inactives (4 per cent) were either officials or committee members in their voluntary associations.[30]

As well as looking at the steelworkers' participation in non-union voluntary associations, the survey also attempted to measure the nature and overall level of their social interaction, including both formal and informal kinds. Thus the respondents were asked which of a list of specified social activities they had taken part in during the week preceding the interview and how often they had taken part in each one they selected. The respondents were also asked if they had taken part in any social activities not included in the list; if so, to say what these were and the number of times they had taken part in each.

Table 3.6   *Number of social activities respondents took part in in the week preceding interview*

Number of social activities	Inactive %	Active %
0 – 3	39.0	18.5
4 – 7	27.1	38.5
8 – 11	18.6	26.2
12 – 15	8.5	9.2
16 – 19	5.1	6.2
20 or more	1.7	1.5
Total	100 (N = 59)	100 (N = 65[a])

[a] One respondent was on holiday during the week preceding the interview and was therefore not asked this question.

Note: 1-tailed K–S test P = 0.05, G = 0.24.

First, the total amounts of social activities undertaken by the respondents through-out this week were assessed as shown in Table 3.6. Here it can be seen that the active respondents undertook a significantly greater number of social activities during the week than the inactives did: the median number undertaken by the actives was in fact 7 and that for the inactives 5. However, the degree of association between social activity in general and union activity was on the low side.[31]

Secondly, in the steelworkers' response to the question of their social interaction, the type of social activities they took part in were examined. Table A3.4 shows the active and inactive members' most popular social activities to be very similar to each others' and of an informal nature in general. The most popular social activity was going to the pub (enjoyed by 58 per cent of the actives and 70 per cent of the in-actives), with going to a workingman's club following close behind. Calling on people and being visited by people occupied the next two places in the popularity listing. Although the remaining types of social activity were undertaken by smaller numbers of respondents, it is worth noting that going out to watch a match of some kind was more popular among the active than the inactive respondents (31 per cent com-pared to 8 per cent), a point that ties up, as we shall see later, with the actives' generally greater active interest in sport. The more frequent attendance by active members of a club or society meeting in the week preceding the interview obviously reflects their greater participation in non-union formal associations; their more frequent attendance of a trade union function of some kind is self-explanatory.

It was also relevant in investigating this topic to see whether the active, despite his undertaking so much more social activity both inside and outside the union branch, still managed to have as many hobbies and interests and to spend as much time with his family as the inactive did. Accordingly, we asked our respondents what were their hobbies and what did they do in their spare time generally. A long and varied list of examples was given here, including ways of spending spare time that respondents might not have thought of mentioning, such as watching television or working on the car. The results of this question are given in Table A3.5. They show that the actives had as many and as great a variety of spare-time interests and hobbies as had the inactives. It is interesting to note that the one spare-time interest, where actives and inactives differed significantly in the extent to which they mentioned it, was that which demanded the most activity in a physical sense: well over a third of the actives (38 per cent) took part in sport of some kind as a spare-time interest compared to only 15 per cent of the inactives.[32] Taking active and inactive respondents together the most popular interest or hobby was clearly gardening: half of both groups mentioned it. The next most popular interests and hobbies were working on the car, 'do-it-yourself', following football, watching television and going to the pub: about a quarter to a third of the respondents in both groups mentioned these items.

To see whether the active respondents spent as much time with their families as the inactive ones, two extra items were added to the end of the list of social activities used in the interview to measure the respondent's level of social activity during the week preceding the interview. These were 'went shopping with the wife' and 'took the children to do or see something'. The items were asked of all those with wives and all those with dependent children.[33] The last two categories of Table A3.4 demonstrate that the active members took part in these family activities at least as frequently as did the inactives.

The final testing of the 'social activity' theory to be examined in this chapter concerns the extent of the active and inactive steelworkers' friendship circles. Two kinds of social acquaintances were included here – workmates and leisure-time companions. With regard to workmates, we have already seen in the discussion of the survey evidence relating to the 'stake-in-the-job' theory that the active members were a little more likely to consider some of the people they worked with as 'close friends' than were the inactives. The same appears to be the case for leisure-time companions. When the steelworkers were asked in the survey the question 'Whom do you most often spend your spare time with?', the number of friends to be so named was not specified and, in fact, most respondents named between one and four. A comparison of the numbers named by the active and inactive respondents shows the active ones to be again a little more likely (though not significantly and suggestively so in statistical terms) to name more; thus 53 per cent of the actives named more than three companions compared to 39 per cent of the inactives (see Table A3.6).

Some conclusions regarding the survey's empirical verification of the more tangible aspects of the 'social activity' theory of branch participation can now be drawn. The contention that the active took a greater part than the inactive member in non-union voluntary associations was well supported. However, the relationships between activity on the one hand and level of social interaction and number of social acquaintances on the other, although both positive, tended to be weak relative to other findings in the survey. This evidence suggests that actives, both younger and older, possessed a slightly higher outward sociability drive than inactive members, retaining at the same time as many 'spare time' interests as their inactive counterparts and seeing as much of their families.[34] But this sociability drive cannot adequately explain the participation pattern evident in the two branches covered by the survey. Moreover, the moderately strong relationship between participation in other voluntary associations and branch activity is capable of alternative interpretation, as will be seen later.

Survey findings relevant to the 'technological implication' approach

The survey hoped to answer the question 'Were the activity patterns of the individual branch members influenced by the way in which their work tasks and roles were defined by the technological layout of the steelworks?'. More specifically, 'Did the active members have greater job accessibility than the inactives and did activity tend to cluster by department or rota?'.[35]

To measure the respondent's degree of job accessibility, the respondents were asked the question 'Some jobs allow people to talk to each other more than others depending on how near you work to other people, how noisy the place is, how much you have to concentrate, how much walking about you do, how much talking to other people can you do while you are working?'. No difference was found between the actives' and inactives' choice of reply: both groups divided themselves fairly evenly among the five category choices which ranged from 'a very great deal' to 'hardly at all'.

With regard to rota, there was no difference either in the Melting Shop or in the Bloom and Billet Mill as to which rota the actives and inactives belonged to. Nor was there any difference between the two groups in the Bloom and Billet Mill as to which department they belonged to. In the Melting Shop, however, there did initially appear to be a tendency for actives and inactives to belong to different departments. The actives, in fact, tended to be drawn from the Furnace and Casting Bays (34 out of 44; 77 per cent) and the inactives from the Mould Preparation Bay (8 out of 13; 62 per cent).[36] However, when skill level was controlled, the relationship did not hold, the general level of skill being higher in the Furnace and Casting Bays and skill, as we have seen previously, was positively related to activity. In fact the mean job percentage bonus ratings of the Furnace and Casting Bays were 66.4 per cent and 61.1 per cent, whereas the corresponding figure for the Mould Preparation Bay was 52.4 per cent and there were no jobs in the latter department with ratings over 55 per cent. There was considerably less skill distinction between departments in the Bloom and Billet Mill.[37] Thus it can be argued here that the departmental distinction in activity suggested by the survey is merely a reflection of differences in departmental skill levels. Consequently, it is possible to maintain that none of the survey findings discussed in this section support contentions of the technological implications approach to branch participation.

This chapter has concentrated on relating the findings in the survey of British steelworkers to the more tangible and measurable contentions in the various US theories of local participation. None of these theories has had enough of its more factual contentions established beyond dispute to suggest that it will be a satisfactory guide when we come to the more intangible and complex questions of perception and motivation in the next chapter. It seems clear that a new approach is needed to account *fully* for the phenomenon of branch participation in Great Britain and this I will try to develop in the next chapter.

4

THE EMERGENCE OF A COMMITMENT TO COLLECTIVISM THEORY

The most important component in any theory of branch or local participation – the survey results concerning which have not yet been discussed – is the active's perception of the purposes of trade unionism and his motivation for taking part. Thus for the 'stake-in-the-job' theory the crucial link between the active's high stake and his participation was his view of the primary function of trade unionism as performing certain vital functions to protect his interests. I wanted to focus in this investigation, however, on the idea that participation can be based on a commitment to collectivism, an idea which has been seriously neglected by many writers on trade union participation. Such an approach would, I suggest, be based on the following premises:

(1)   The group which the active member views as the basis for collective action can vary from the shop or plant at one end of a continuum to workers in general at the other. The type of group ends the active member is concerned with can also vary along a continuum from very specific economic issues at one end to broad social and political goals at the other. Finally, the type of belief in collectivism can also vary along a continuum from an instrumental belief at one end, where the collective action is seen as a means to the achievement of the active member's private goals (such as the economic advance of himself and his nuclear family), through an intrinsic belief in collectivism, where collective action is seen as a means to ends conceived as the goals of trade unionism as a social movement (such as the improvement in workers' share in society in Britain), to solidaristic belief at the other, where participation in collectivism is seen as an end in itself.

(2)   The active member believes that trade unionism can achieve, or help to achieve, these valued ends or goals; thus trade union participation represents the rational pursuit of important objectives and cherished ideals. The active is prepared to bear the costs of his participation to his other roles (such as familial or leisure), because of the value he attaches to the achievement of these group ends. Where collectivism is an end in itself, participation is not experienced as a cost at all but is itself a source of rewards of a kind not otherwise obtainable.

(3)   However, a commitment to collectivism does not exist in isolation; individuals have, at least to some extent, coherent systems of values and beliefs. Not surprisingly then, one finds in the literature that does cover the question of commitment to trade unionism, that the authors also frequently include

| Table 4.1 | Reasons for respondents' first joining a trade union (respondents could give more than one reason) | | |

Reason	Inactive %	Active %
(1) Intrinsic belief or deep interest in trade unionism	3.4	43.9
(2) Instrumental belief on the collective level	5.1	10.6
(3) Instrumental belief on the individual level	52.5	30.3
(4) All workmates were members, joined because asked to	16.9	6.1
(5) Coercion due to closed shop	22.0	10.6
(6) Influence of branch official or family	5.1	0
(7) Other	1.7	1.5
	(N = 59)	(N = 66)

Notes: Intrinsic belief v. other reasons, X^2, test P = 0.001, θ = 0.54.
Instrumental individual level v. other reasons, X^2 test P = 0.01, θ = 0.23
No positive motivations (4) + (5) v. other reasons, X^2 test P = 0.05, θ = 0.28.

descriptions of all or some of the features of the active members' social imagery, their views on the relationship between men and management in society and their degree of support of (perhaps including activity in) political parties. Thus a commitment to trade unionism appears to be part of a general 'sociopolitical orientation', which the inactive members either do not share or do not share to the same extent. It is contended here that the active members' commitment to collectivism is only fully understandable when seen in the context of this larger pattern of attitudes and behaviour.

In this chapter, the findings of the survey of steel workers' motives for joining a trade union and for taking or not taking part, as the case may be, in branch affairs will be discussed first, together with the steelworkers' views on various aspects of trade unionism. In particular, attention will be paid to their views on striking, the role of trade unions in present-day industrial, political and social life and the role of trade unions in social change. Secondly, the survey's findings on the steelworkers' image of society will be reviewed, including their perception of the relationship between management and men in today's society and their degree of satisfaction with the present social structure, together with the steelworkers' choice of political party and general interest in political affairs.

The steelworkers' motives for participation and their perception of trade unionism

We shall consider, first of all, the reasons the steelworkers gave in reply to the survey's open-ended question on why they first joined a trade union. These answers are summarised in Table 4.1, which shows that the active members were much more likely than the inactive to refer to their intrinsic beliefs in trade unionism

Table 4.2   *Reasons given by active respondents for first becoming active in a trade union branch (respondents could give more than one reason)*

Reason	Number	%
(1) Intrinsic belief or deep interest in trade unionism	34	51.5
(2) Instrumental belief on the collective level	24	36.4
(3) Instrumental belief on the individual level	7	10.6
(4) 'Like to know what's going off'	4	6.1
(5) Opportunities for social life or for helping people	2	3.0
(6) Influence of family	5	7.6
(7) Influence of workmates or branch officials	4	6.1
(8) Had a 'suitable' job	1	1.5
(9) 'Accidentally' became active	5	7.6
(10) Other (e.g. had the spare time)	2	3.0
		(N = 66)

as their reason for joining their first trade union, and that the degree of association between giving intrinsic belief as a reason for joining and activity was moderately high.[1]

In contrast, the inactives were significantly more likely to say they joined in order to benefit themselves personally, some in terms of gaining fringe benefits, some in terms of job protection. The degree of association here was, however, lower than that found previously between activity and intrinsic belief. This indicates that while some at least of the steelworkers first joined a trade union in order to protect and enhance their job interests, this kind of answer was not restricted to active members but, in fact, was more commonly given by the inactives. The inactives were also significantly more likely to give reasons that displayed no positive motivation on their own behalf: that is they joined because everybody else in the shop was a member, because they were asked to they simply did so without thinking about it, or because they were forced to by the existence of a closed shop. In fact 39 per cent of inactives gave reasons of this type compared to 17 per cent of the actives and the degree of association here was similar to that in the previous case.

The most obvious question to ask the active respondents in a study of the characteristics and motivation of branch actives is 'Why are you active?', yet at the same time this type of question is perhaps the most difficult on which to get meaningful replies. The active may rationalise his replies or he may deliberately conceal his true reasons for activity if he suspects them not to be socially approved. The active respondents were asked two open-ended questions here on their motivation to take part in branch affairs. They were asked first to describe to the interviewer how they first became active in a union branch and, secondly, why they continued to be active in their present BISAKTA branch.

The classification of the descriptions given by the actives for their first becoming active are given in Table 4.2. Again, by far the largest category in this table – and increased in size from Table 4.1 – consisted of those actives who emphasised the role of their intrinsic belief in unionism. For the majority of these actives, their intrinsic belief appears to have led directly to their becoming active as soon as they joined their first trade union or after they had been branch members for a short period. However, five of the 34 actives involved here, as well as referring to their intrinsic beliefs in trade unionism, also mentioned an incident that had occurred or the experience of a particular situation that had 'jogged' them into actually participating. These incidents were concerned with aspects of the material welfare of these actives and their fellow workers, such as wages, working conditions or problems of redundancy. Thus these five workers' accounts of becoming active led to their being placed in two categories in Table 4.2: category (2) as well as category (1).

Two examples of an active's beliefs leading him straight from joining into becoming active in a trade union branch are given below.

Respondent 1

Interviewer: Why did you join a union in the first place?

Respondent: As I say, well, I joined the union because obviously as far as my views are it's the union for the workman to be in. I think that as far as this is concerned it's the obvious solution is for the men to be represented, to put their views as the negotiating body to the management instead of speaking as individuals.

Interviewer: Why did you first become active in the branch, what started you off?

Respondent: Well I don't know any particular isolated point which started me off, well I simply thought that if you joined something you take an interest in it, and you participate in it, it is as simple as that.

Interviewer: Why did you become so interested in trade unionism?

Respondent: Well I think the main reason is pure and simple, there was a period in between the wars I think, the working man had no voice at all as regards putting views forward to management and country as a whole, and therefore I believe working men should be in a body to present one's opinion as far as the majority of a lot of people are concerned so management knows what the views are of the bulk of its workers.

Respondent 2   (explaining how his interest led him into becoming active)

Well actually I came active straight away like. I started going to union meetings as soon as they started union meetings after I joined and I've carried on from there like. I've collected money here like and go to every meeting I can. I worked on a rota so I couldn't get there sometimes but apart from that I don't miss one.

The next largest group of actives in Table 4.2 gave accounts of their becoming active which referred to the attainment of material benefits for themselves and their fellow workers. Of the 24 actives here, five (as we have seen) also referred to their

34

intrinsic belief in trade unionism. However of the other 19 who did not, only four referred to a belief in trade unionism of a limited instrumental kind. The remaining 15 actives in category (2) gave accounts of their first becoming active which prominently featured experience of an incident or particular situation concerned with the material welfare of workers in their shop, plant or firm, which led to their taking up branch participation on a permanent basis. Excerpts from three active respondents' accounts of such incidents are given below.

> When I first started there, (another large steel firm in Sheffield) wages were lower than what I'd had before for same hours and we were working just as hard, and chap that were running branch, he were councillor, he were a J.P., a member of the Fire Brigade committee, a lot of other commitments. He didn't seem to be doing as much as he could for the branch and I ended up getting job from him and I lifted money up a lot. We kept going in and getting prices for jobs and that.

> It were through conditions being so bad there at X (another large steel firm in Sheffield). I had to join a union in the first place as it was a condition of work there. And through joining, I realised what was happening – bad conditions, bad pay – and instead of thinking someone ought to do it, I thought I ought to do something about it and I took an active part. (I jumped) into the shop steward's job and a year after I was made secretary.

> My interest in trade unions first stemmed through employees being persecuted and I decided there and then that some power must be displayed by someone in the local branch in the mines. I kept up this interest for quite a while and I was appointed delegate in this branch in the mines.

A smaller number of active respondents were classified in Table 4.2 as having become active through instrumental reasons related to their own individual interests and not to those of other workers in their shop, or workers in general. However, three out of the seven actives here referred as before to the occurrence of a specific incident or situation in which they were involved and which led them to become active on a permanent basis, and not to any belief in trade unionism as a means of enhancing and protecting job interests.

An active's account of a specific incident concerning his own interests that led to his becoming permanently active is given below:

> My first union experience was once when the manager told me I couldn't go to school. They'd stopped my schooling because I wouldn't work overtime; the union said there was no overtime. I wouldn't work overtime so the manager said he'd stop my schooling and we had a bit of a meeting outside the firm and the shop steward went in and he straightened it out . . . . that's how I first became interested in trade unions.

Finally, we can note that five actives in Table 4.2 described their becoming active as accidental, often through pressure of their fellow members. One respondent's description of such an 'accident' is given below:

> Well, at one branch meeting I was told that there was nobody representing

Table 4.3   *Reasons given by active respondents for*
continuing to be active in their present
trade union branch (respondents could
give more than one reason)

Reason	Number	%
(1) Intrinsic belief or deep interest in trade unionism	43	65.2
(2) Instrumental belief on the collective level	10	15.2
(3) Instrumental belief on the individual level	10	15.2
(4) 'Like to know what's going off'	14	21.2
(5) Opportunities for social life	4	6.1
(6) Sense of achievement	1	1.5
(7) Other	1	1.5
		(N = 66)

the crane drivers because working on the rota system, you know, that we used to work on and we saw the union man perhaps every three weeks or something like that, and it was suggested that I put my name down to re-present the crane drivers when there was nobody else present, which I did.

The importance of the experience of incidents/particular situations in the steel-workers' accounts of their instrumental reasons for becoming active, and the way in which these actives become active so readily and continued to participate so steadily afterwards, suggests that 18 of the 26 actives who were classified as giving instru-mental-type reasons of some kind but who did not directly refer to any intrinsic belief in trade unionism, had in fact some kind of underlying intrinsic belief that was 'triggered off' by their experience. Since the proportion of actives giving instrumental reasons of some kind for joining and for becoming active is roughly the same (44 per cent and 47 per cent respectively), it can also be argued that a 'collective incident' is more effective in triggering off an underlying intrinsic belief than an 'individual' one. Again the five actives who so readily became 'accidentally' active and so con-sistently remained active after their 'accident' can also reasonably be included among those with an underlying intrinsic belief that was 'triggered off' by some event. This makes a total of 23 actives out of the 66 with experience of a belief-precipitating event of some kind. Indeed, as we shall see in the next chapter, some of the influences that are likely to have predisposed the actives towards a belief in trade unionism, e.g. influence of family of origin, must necessarily have occurred before the actives themselves even joined a trade union.

The classification of the reasons the actives gave for continuing to be active in their present branch is shown in Table 4.3. Here we can see that the intrinsic belief category was once more the most frequently referred to, but the number of actives involved has now increased to nearly two-thirds. When we consider the smaller pro-portion of actives in this table giving instrumental-type reasons, it confirms the view that, while some of the steelworkers may have become active through material considerations, they did not continue to be active because of a belief in trade unionism of a strictly limited instrumental kind, nor because of a belief that participation was

Table 4.4   *Reasons given by inactive respondents for others' taking part in branch affairs (respondents could give more than one reason)*

Reason	Number	%
(1) Intrinsic belief or deep interest in trade unionism	29	49.2
(2) Instrumental belief on the collective level	6	10.2
(3) Instrumental belief on the individual level	10	16.9
(4) Possession of socially approved personality traits (e.g. 'It's in them to lead people')	6	10.2
(5) Possession of socially disapproved personality traits (e.g. 'They're noisy shouters who like to exercise power')	6	10.2
(6) Other	3	5.1
(7) No particular reason	12	20.3
		($N = 59$)

a rational means of protecting and enhancing an individual's job interests. But instead they tended to be motivated to continue their activity by their newly-awakened intrinsic belief in the goals of trade unionism. In a similar fashion, those who 'accidentally' became active tended to carry on their participation through their newly-awakened instrinsic belief in collectivism.

The category that has changed most noticeably in Table 4.3 from Table 4.2, and which did not even feature in Table 4.1, consisted of those active respondents who explained their present level of participation in the branch as due to their 'liking to know what's going off', as the steelworkers expressed it. Just under a quarter appeared to enjoy and value being involved in events taking place in the branch, influencing decisions being made and knowing what was happening, as experiences in themselves. Seven of the actives here, in fact, combined their intrinsic belief and a 'liking to know what's going off' in accounting for their present participation.

One of the reasons for being active, that a branch member might conceal in the interview for fear of social disapproval, is the ambition to become a full-time trade union official, thus using the holding of branch office as a stepping-stone to a career in the union hierarchy. In an attempt to counter this, the active respondents were asked a separate question in the interview on whether they would like to have a full-time union job or not. In fact just over a quarter of the actives – 17 out of 66 – replied that they would like to be a full-time trade union official, whereas none of the actives had previously mentioned it as a reason for their becoming or continuing to be active. Indeed, the actives appear to have given some thought to the matter, since half of those who would like to become full-time officials mentioned what were to them the attractive features of the job, such as the interest and responsibility involved and the opportunity to meet people and find out about different points of view. However, it is possible there was some extent of exaggeration of the actives' ambitions here.[2]

Another reason for their participation that the actives may have concealed is the

Table 4.5   *Reasons given by inactive respondents for*
            their not taking part in branch affairs
            (respondents could give more than one reason)

Reason	Number	%
(1) Not interested in trade unionism/ branch affairs	28	47.5
(2) Other activities (domestic and leisure) take up too much time	18	30.5
(3) Lack of ability or education	8	13.5
(4) Critical of branch leadership	3	5.1
(5) Other	2	3.4
		$(N = 59)$

desire for promotion to a management position. But as we saw previously in reply to a separate question on wanting to be a foreman, most actives preferred to stay on the shop floor anyway. In fact, only five actives (3 per cent) had replied that they would like to become a foreman 'very much indeed'.

In considering the possibility that the actives concealed in the interview some of their reasons for their participation, the inactive respondents were asked why they thought some people took an active part in the branch (on the assumption that while the actives might be able successfully to fool an interviewer in an hour-long interview, they would not be able to fool their workmates who saw a great deal more of them). Table 4.4 gives a summary of the inactive respondents' replies to the open-ended question 'Why do you think some people do take an active part in the branch?'. Here we can see that almost half of the inactives saw intrinsic belief or deep interest in trade unionism as the motivating force in branch activity, just as the actives themselves had stressed in accounting both for their becoming and for their continuing to be active. An additional 10 per cent of the inactives thought that the actives sought benefits for all of the workers in their group or branch. Only a small proportion of the inactives thought that the actives were motivated by self interest and indeed, this tallies with the previous finding that some of the actives admitted participating for such reasons. None of the inactives considered that the actives were motivated by ambition to become a full-time union official and this indicates that the extent of union ambition among the actives as revealed by the survey's direct question on it was, as suggested previously, exaggerated to some extent.

The inactive respondents in the survey were also asked in an open-ended fashion why they did not take an active part in the branch. Their replies are summarised in Table 4.5. Here we can see that the most important reason for not taking part was that they were not interested in trade unionism: in other words they lacked the actives' sense of commitment to collectivism. The next most important reason was that they did not have the spare time to take part in branch affairs. The previous finding, that the active steelworkers despite spending time on branch affairs still managed to have as many interests and hobbies as the inactive steelworkers and to spend as much time with their families, suggests that the inactives who gave this type of reason were simply concealing their lack of interest.

The next set of survey findings to be considered are the steelworkers' attitudes towards striking. It was a point of central interest in the survey to see if the active and

Table 4.6   *Respondents' attitudes towards striking in general*

Response chosen	(i) All respondents		(ii) Respondents aged under 40 years		(iii) Respondents aged 40 years and over	
	Inactive %	Active %	Inactive %	Active %	Inactive %	Active %
(1) I would go on strike if the union called one, but I personally wouldn't want to	45.8	21.2	38.7	20.8	53.6	21.4
(2) I would willingly go on strike if the union called one which I considered necessary	44.1	54.5	45.2	54.2	42.9	54.8
(3) I would go on strike if I considered it necessary, whether or not the union approved	10.2	22.7	16.1	25.0	3.6	21.4
(4) Don't know	0	1.5	0	0	0	2.4
Total	100 (N=59)	100 (N=66)	100 (N=31)	100 (N=24)	100 (N=28)	100 (N=42)

Notes: Column (i)   K–S test excluding (4) P = 0.10 G = 0.45
      Column (ii)   K–S test excluding (4) P > 0.10 G = 0.32
      Column (iii) K–S test excluding (4) P = 0.10 G = 0.62

inactive steelworkers differed in their degree of militancy and how this was related to their motivation to participate. To this end, the respondents were asked two questions in the interview, one concerned with their attitudes towards striking in general terms and the other with the more specific issue of sympathy striking.

The steelworkers' choice of replies to the question on how they felt about strikes in general is given in Table 4.6. Column (i) of this table shows the actives as a group to be significantly more militant than the inactive members: over half of the actives said they would willingly go out on strike if their union called one which they considered necessary and, in addition, nearly a quarter said they would go on strike if they considered it necessary, even if their union disapproved. In contrast, almost half of the inactives said they would not be personally willing to go on strike, and a smaller proportion than was the case for the actives said they were willing to support a union-called strike. The degree of association here between having a more militant attitude to striking and activity was moderately high.

However, when age was controlled for, it was found that the degree of association between general willingness to strike and activity decreased for the younger respondents and increased for the older respondents as can be seen in columns (ii) and (iii) of Table 4.6. This difference between the two age groups was brought about by substantial differences in the proportions of the older and younger inactives who were, in general, willing to go on strike (46 per cent compared to 61 per cent). The proportions of older and younger actives so willing were in fact very similar: 76 per cent and 79 per cent respectively. Thus the older actives were relatively more militant than their inactive counterparts, whereas the younger actives were not.

On the issue of sympathy striking, the respondents were asked the open-ended question 'How do you feel about going on strike in support of workers at other plants?'. The respondents' replies were coded for general agreement or disagreement and the results are shown in Table 4.7. Column (i) of this table shows that in the case of this more controversial issue, there were no overall differences between the active and inactive respondents: the majority of both groups disagreed with such action.

However, when age was controlled for, a significant difference did appear between the older active and inactive respondents with respect to sympathy striking, while the relationship continued to be insignificant for the younger respondents, as columns (ii) and (iii) of Table 4.7 show. Again this difference in the relationship between the older and younger respondents was due to the lack of militancy displayed by the older inactives. The degree of association for the older respondents here, between agreeing with such action and activity, was moderately high similar to that found previously for the older respondents between being willing to go on strike in general and activity.

When discussed previously, in the context of respondents attitudes towards management, the survey finding that the propensity to take up grievances was relatively strong related to activity, it was suggested that this finding, on account of its discrepancy from other findings on the respondents' attitudes towards management, fitted in better with findings here on attitudes towards striking. This seems to be the most plausible interpretation of the survey findings, although the degree of association between the propensity to take up grievances and activity (0.59) was somewhat higher than that found here between being more militant and active

Table 4.7   Respondents' attitudes towards sympathy striking

Attitude	(i) All		(ii) Respondents aged under 40 years		(iii) Respondents aged 40 years or more	
	Inactive %	Active %	Inactive %	Active %	Inactive %	Active %
(1) Agrees in general	32.2	42.4	45.2	37.5	17.9	45.2
(2) Disagrees in general	57.6	54.5	45.2	62.5	71.4	50.0
(3) Other	8.5	1.5	9.7	0	7.1	2.4
(4) Don't know	1.7	1.5	0	0	3.6	2.4
Total	100 (N=59)	100 (N=66)	100 (N=31)	100 (N=24)	100 (N=28)	100 (N=42)

Notes: Column (i) X^2 test (1) v. (2) to (4) P > 0.10
Column (ii) X^2 test (1) v. (2) to (4) P > 0.10
Column (iii) X^2 test (1) v. (2) to (4) P = 0.05, G = 0.58

(0.45), and although in propensity to take up grievances there were no differences observed between older and younger steelworkers. Thus it can be be argued that just as the active respondents are more prepared than the inactives to take collective action of a moderate nature to acquire the goals they believe trade unions should pursue, so they are also much more prepared to make use of collective channels for airing their own individual grievances.

We turn now to consider the steelworkers' views as to the proper role of trade unions in present-day industrial and political life and in workers' social lives. The respondents were asked first here in the interview what part they felt trade unions should play in British industrial life; they were then handed a card giving a choice of six different role sizes including a 'don't know' category and asked to choose the one they considered most appropriate. Secondly, if they thought that the trade union should play at least a small part, they were asked as an open-ended question 'What do you think trade unions in general and your branch in particular should try and achieve in the industrial area?'. Similar procedures were followed to obtain the respondents' views on the role of trade unions in British political life and in workers' social lives. Column (i) of Table 4.8 gives the results for the questions on the size of trade unions' role in industrial, political and social affairs. Here we can see that, while the majority of both active and inactive groups felt that trade unions should play a very important part indeed in industrial life, the proportion of active respondents so feeling was significantly greater and the degree of association here between so thinking and activity was moderately high. When age was controlled for, differences were found in the relationship between opinion on size of union industrial role and activity for the younger and older respondents, as columns (ii) and (iii) of this table show. The degree of association increased for the younger respondents to a relatively high level, while the relationship between the two variables was not significant for the older respondents. This difference was due, not to the younger actives' having a greater conception of trade union role in the industrial area than the older actives, but to the younger inactives being much less likely than the older inactives to give such an answer.[3]

Although the active members had a greater conception than the inactive ones of trade unions' role in industry, there were no differences between the two groups in their endorsement of the specific goals they felt trade unions should pursue in this general area: both groups felt trade unions should seek the improvement of present industrial conditions for workers. The most frequently cited goal was the improvement of wages, put forward by 67 per cent (44 out of 66) of the actives and by 51 per cent (30 out of 59) of the inactives. Better working conditions was put forward by 45 per cent (32) of the actives and by 41 per cent (24) of the inactives, and looking after workers' interests in general by 14 per cent (9) of the actives and 8 per cent (5) of the inactives. Only 12 per cent (8) of the actives and 10 per cent (6) of the inactives felt the purpose of trade unions in industrial life was to protect and enhance a worker's vested interest in his job, and only an additional 3 per cent (2) of the actives and 5 per cent (3) of the inactives felt that the central concern of trade unions should be the processing of individual worker's grievances. Again, only 8 per cent (5) of the actives and 3 per cent (2) of the inactives felt trade unions should concern themselves with changing the present wage system: indeed a further substantial minority of both groups, 24 per cent (16) of the actives and 29 per cent

Table 4.8   Respondents' conception of the role of trade unions in present-day society

| Extent of role trade unions should play | Industrial life | | | | | | (iv) Political life | | (v) Social life | |
| | (i) All respondents | | (ii) Respondents under 40 years | | (iii) Respondents aged 40 years or more | | | | | |
	Inactive %	Active %	Inactive %	Active %	Inactive %	Active %	Inactive %	Active %	Inactive %	Active %
(1) Very important part	52.5	80.3	38.7	79.2	67.9	81.0	13.6	28.8	5.1	9.1
(2) Pretty important part	25.4	16.7	32.3	20.8	17.9	14.3	20.3	18.2	3.4	12.1
(3) Part of some importance	20.3	1.5	25.8	0	14.3	2.4	23.7	24.2	13.6	12.1
(4) Only a small part	0	1.5	0	0	0	2.4	18.6	9.1	28.8	24.2
(5) No part at all	1.7	1.5	3.2	0	0	0	20.3	18.2	49.2	42.4
(6) Don't know	0	0	0	0	0	0	3.4	1.5	0	0
Total	100 (N=59)	100 (N=66)	100 (N=31)	100 (N=24)	100 (N=28)	100 (N=42)	100 (N=59)	100 (N=66)	100 (N=59)	100 (N=66)

Notes: Column (i) X^2 test (1) v. (2) to (5) P = 0.01, G = 0.57.
Column (ii) X^2 test (1) v. (2) to (5) P = 0.01, G = 0.74.
Column (iii) X^2 test (1) v. (2) to (5) P > 0.10.
Column (iv) X^2 test (1) v. (2) to (5) P = 0.10, G = 0.22.
Column (v) X^2 test (1) + (2) v. (3) to (5) P = 0.10, G = 0.18.

(17) of the inactives, believed the purpose of trade unions to be the 'creation of harmony between management and men'.[4]

An additional question was asked here on the very important question of 'the frontier of control' in industry. The respondents were asked whether they felt trade unions should just be concerned with getting higher pay and better conditions for their members, or whether trade unions should also try to get workers a say in management. Here no difference was found between the active and inactive respondents: the majority of both groups – 70 per cent of the active (46 out of 66) and 64 per cent of the inactive (38 out of 59) – thought that trade unions should in fact extend 'the frontier of control' and get workers such a say.[5]

Column (iv) of Table 4.8 shows that both the actives and inactives felt that the trade unions should play a smaller part in political life than in industrial life but, nevertheless, the majority of both groups felt that trade unions should play a part of at least some importance in political life. The actives, however, were suggestively more likely to think that trade unions should play an important part here than were the inactives, although the degree of association was small. The actives also had a very much clearer idea of what specific political aims they wished the trade unions to pursue, although they did not stress any one particular aim.[6] Thirteen per cent of the actives (7 out of 53) and 13 per cent also of the inactives (6 out of 45) mentioned working cooperatively with the government in office and/or industry; 15 per cent (8) of the actives and 18 per cent (8) of the inactives felt trade unions should work for the reduction of unemployment in general in Britain. Thirteen per cent (7) of the actives and 4 per cent (2) of the inactives cited the 'representation of the working class to the public and government in office', while exactly the same proportions for both groups mentioned supporting the Labour Party or putting trade union members into Parliament. Finally 9 per cent (5) of the actives said trade unions should 'create unity' among all workers.

In the context of the role of trade unions in the political sphere, the steelworkers were also asked for their views on the relationship between trade unions and the Labour Party and whether they contributed to Labour Party funds. The respondents were asked first whether the trade unions should support the Labour Party or whether they should keep themselves separate. Here no difference was found between the active and inactive respondents. The majority of both groups – 65 per cent of the actives (43 out of 66) and 53 per cent of the inactives (31 out of 59) – were in favour of the historical alliance, while 33 per cent (22) of the actives and 44 per cent (26) of the inactives felt it should come to an end.[7] Secondly, the respondents were asked whether or not they paid the political levy. Those respondents who replied that they did not were further asked if they had 'contracted out'. Since Party dues were automatically deducted from all workers' wages at the steelworks, it can be assumed that all respondents who had not actually contracted out were in fact paying the levy, even if they replied that they were not. The results of the question are given in Table 4.9. Here we can see that a much greater proportion of the actives than of the inactives *knowingly* paid the political levy: a surprisingly high proportion of the inactives (76 per cent) did not know whether, or were unaware that, they paid it. The degree of association here between knowingly paying the levy and activity was moderate.

Both groups of respondents felt that the trade unions should play a smaller role in

Table 4.9   *Respondents' payment of the political levy*

	Inactive %	Active %
(1) Respondent replied that he did pay the levy	20.3	54.5
(2) Respondent replied that he did not pay the levy and had contracted out	3.4	4.5
(3) Respondent replied that he did not pay the levy but had not contracted out	67.8	33.3
(4) Respondent did not know if he paid the levy or not	8.5	7.6
Total	100 (N=59)	100 (N=66)

Note: X^2 test (1) *v*. (2) to (4) P = 0.001, θ = 0.39.

workers' social lives than in industrial and political life, as column (v) in Table 4.8 shows; nevertheless, over half of both groups felt that trade unions should play at least a small part in workers' social lives. Again, the actives were suggestively more likely than the inactives to believe that the unions should play a 'very important' or 'pretty important' role here, although the degree of association was very small. Few of the inactive steelworkers had any concrete ideas about what trade unions should seek to achieve in the social sphere. The actives, however, had two basic demands. First, the actives felt that trade unions should provide at least to some extent a social milieu for their members by providing facilities for members to meet and undertake activities with each other – including provision for workers' families – either at the workplace or in the city centre. This aim was mentioned by 47 per cent of the actives involved here (18 out of 38). Second, they felt that trade unions should work for the improvement of public facilities and services; thus trade unions should press for better parks, better education and playground facilities for children, better housing, more help for disadvantaged groups such as old age pensioners and, finally, for the improvement of the quality of life for the worker.[8] This second aim was mentioned by 21 per cent (8) of the actives.

Finally in this section on the steelworkers' motives for participation in and views on trade unionism, their views on the role trade unions should play in future social change will be considered. Table 4.10 summarises the survey findings on this topic.[9] In column (i) we can see that the largest group of active steel workers (42 per cent in all) felt that trade unions should work to improve present society in some way, mainly through the redistribution of income and wealth, while a some-what smaller proportion of them felt trade unions should concentrate on a defensive role and protect present union achievements. The inactive steelworkers, on the other hand, were fairly evenly divided between the redistribution and defensive roles. However, only a small number of active or inactive members thought trade unions should devote themselves to the reconstruction of present society or, con-versely, considered that trade unions had no role to play in the future.

If we look in column (i) of Table 4.10 at the number of actives and inactives

Table 4.10   Respondents' view of the role of trade unions in future social change

	(i) All respondents		(ii) Respondents aged under 40 years		(iii) Respondents aged 40 years and over	
	Inactive %	Active %	Inactive %	Active %	Inactive %	Active %
(1) Reconstructing society	8.5	16.7	9.7	16.7	7.1	16.7
(2) Redistributing income and wealth within present society	30.5	31.8	32.3	20.8	28.6	38.1
(3) Improving present society in relation to some other factor (e.g. getting a shorter working week)	1.7	10.6	0	16.7	3.6	7.1
(4) Defending workers' share in present society	35.6	24.2	32.3	16.7	39.3	28.6
(5) Should play no role.	18.6	16.7	19.4	29.2	17.9	9.5
(6) Don't know	5.1	0	6.5	0	3.6	0
Total	100 (N=59)	100 (N=66)	100 (N=31)	100 (N=24)	100 (N=28)	100 (N=42)

Notes: Column (i) X^2 test (1) to (3) $v.$ (4) to (6) P = 0.10, θ = 0.18.
Column (ii) X^2 test (1) to (3) $v.$ (4) to (6) P > 0.10.
Column (iii) X^2 test (1) to (3) $v.$ (4) to (6) P = 0.10, θ = 0.22.

who felt that trade unions should play a role in *changing* society in some way or other, we find that the actives were in fact suggestively more likely to conceive of such a possibility than were the inactives: 59 per cent of the actives considered the trade unions should play such a role compared to 41 per cent of the inactives. The degree of association was low here, as the percentage differences suggest. But when age was controlled for, some difference emerged in the relationship between the conception of trade unions' appropriate role in the future and activity for the two age groups, as columns (ii) and (iii) of Table 4.10 show. Here, the degree of association increased for the older respondents, while the relationship between the variables was not significant for the younger group. Thus 62 per cent of the older actives compared to 54 per cent of the younger actives felt that the trade unions had a role in future social change.

The survey's findings on the steelworkers' motives for participation and their perception of trade unionism will now be summarised. Table 4.11 compares the reasons given by the actives for first joining a trade union, for first becoming active in a branch and for continuing to be active in their present branch. Here we can see that, in general terms, a belief or a commitment to collectivism clearly outweighs all other reasons. More specifically, we can see that the actives' belief in collectivism was primarily intrinsic rather than instrumental. Moreover, in addition to the 52 per cent of actives shown in the table as persons whose intrinsic beliefs led them to participate in a branch as soon as they became trade union members or after a relatively short period of membership, we should remember that the survey material suggested that the majority of those classified as giving instrumental reasons for becoming active had an underlying intrinsic belief in trade unionism which had been triggered off by the experience of some incident or particular situation.[10] Once having become active, these steelworkers were motivated to carry on their participation by their newly awakened intrinsic belief. The inactives concurred that the actives' primary motivation was a commitment to the intrinsic goals of trade unionism and there was little indication from other survey questions that the actives were concealing any socially reprehensible motives. We should also note from this table that some kind of social motivation appears to play a significant though subsidiary role in the actives' continuing participation, although this is scarcely mentioned in accounts of why actives joined or how they first came to be active in a trade union branch. A number of actives thus appeared to want and enjoy the control of events in the branch for their own sake.

Finally in the context of motivation, we should note that Tables 4.1, 4.2 and 4.3 showed that very few of the actives referred directly to the influence of 'significant others' in their lives in explaining their participation, such as the influence of members of their families, leisure time companions or workmates. And few or no respondents referred to the opportunities for social life that participation might offer, to the satisfaction of any psychological needs, or to any technological features of their work tasks and roles that facilitated their participation.

In the investigation of attitudes towards striking, it appeared from the survey results that the actives were significantly more in favour of collective action than were the inactives, particularly so in the case of older respondents. However, only a minority of either active or inactive steelworkers were willing to endorse more militant collective action such as unofficial or sympathy striking. This finding is in

Table 4.11   *Comparison of reasons given by the active respondents for first joining a trade union, for first becoming active in a branch and for continuing to be active in their present branch (respondents could give more than one reason)*

Reason	(i) For first joining	(ii) For first becoming active	(iii) For continuing to be active
	%	%	%
(1) Intrinsic belief or deep interest in trade unionism	43.9 ⎫	51.5 ⎫	65.2 ⎫
(2) Instrumental belief on the collective level	13.6 ⎬ 57.5	36.4 ⎬ 80.3[a]	15.2 ⎬ 77.3[a]
(3) Instrumental belief on the individual level	30.3 ⎭	10.6 ⎭	15.2 ⎭
(4) 'Like to know what's going off'	0	6.1	24.6
	(N=66)	(N=66)	(N=66)

[a] Adjusted for double counting.

line with the previous survey finding on the actives' greater propensity to take up individual grievances with the union.

With regard to the perception of trade unionism, it appears that the actives conceived of the trade unions as playing a larger role in industrial life than did the inactives and, furthermore, that the actives were more likely to endorse political and social roles for trade unions – although these latter two roles were not considered to be as important as the industrial role. The inactive members' ideas on the specific goals trade unions should pursue in political and social life were not sufficiently coherent for them to be compared to those of the actives. But in the context of industrial life, active and inactive members opted for the same specific goals. However, in specifying these goals – the improvement of wages and working conditions were the two most frequently mentioned – the steelworkers did not include any mention of controlling their jobs, despite the previous emphasis on the instrumental/ individual aspect by a third of the actives and half of the inactives in explaining why they first joined a union. On the other hand, both active and inactive members, in reply to a specific question, felt that trade unions should achieve more collective control over the workplace by having more say in management. Finally we can conclude here that an analysis of the kind of economic, political and social trade union goals advocated by the active steelworkers shows their concern with the improvement of society, rather than with radical social change; thus they emphasised such concepts as 'fairation', 'cooperation' and 'representation'.

Finally on the question of perception of the functions of trade unions, the survey showed the actives, mainly the older ones, to be significantly more likely to believe that trade unions should play a part of some kind in the bringing about of future social change, the redistribution of income and wealth within present society being the most popular choice of role.

The steelworkers' images of society and their accompanying political attitudes and behaviour

Table 4.12 gives a breakdown of the active and inactive steelworkers' various images of present-day society – which were obtained from an unstructured discussion on the social structure of present-day society held during the interview – following Cousins and Brown's useful classification.[11] This table shows that the actives' images of society were significantly more likely to correspond to Type A than were those of the inactives. Thus nearly half of the actives compared to just over a tenth of the inactives saw society as consisting of two classes: one a small elite of bosses, managers and property owners and the other, a large conglomerate consisting of everybody else, including themselves. The inactives, instead, divided themselves fairly evenly among the other four types, all of which subdivide today's society into more than two groups. The degree of association between holding a dichotomous image of society and activity was moderately high.

Column (i) of Table 4.13 gives the criteria used by the steelworkers to distinguish between social classes. Here we can see the inactives were significantly more likely than the actives to refer to money, possessions, wages and standard of living: the degree of association between using money as a criterion and inactivity was moderate. The actives were, instead, fairly evenly split between the material criteria above and the more ideologically orientated criterion of the ownership of property and business

Table 4.12   *Respondents' images of present-day society*

Type of image	Inactive %	Active %
(1) Type A	11.9	48.5
(2) Type B	22.0	13.6
(3) Type C	22.0	12.1
(4) Type D	20.3	6.1
(5) Type E	15.3	13.6
(6) 'There are no classes today'	1.7	6.1
(7) No image	6.8	0
Total	100	100
	(N=59)	(N=66)

Note: X^2 test (1) *v.* (2) to (7), P = 0.001, θ = 0.43.

and the ability to live on unearned income. The above were in fact suggestively more likely than the inactives to refer to this ideological criterion. The degree of association, however, between mentioning this factor and activity was low.[12] Those actives with Type A images were particularly likely to refer to the ideological criterion as column (ii) of Table 4.13 shows.

One particularly important aspect of the respondents' conception of the class structure is the extent to which they perceive the classes' interests as clashing and their image of the relationship between men and management in society generally. An analysis of the data from the unstructured discussions on class showed that roughly half of both active and inactive steelworkers – 55 per cent and 50 per cent respectively – felt that some conflict of interests did exist between the classes in society today while just under half – 45 per cent and 50 per cent respectively – felt it did not.[13]

The steelworkers' perception of some degree of class conflict existing in society is confirmed by their agreement/disagreement with the first three statements listed in Table 4.14. Thus the majority of both actives and inactives agreed that 'Big business has too much power in this country' and that 'There is one law for the rich and one for the poor', and disagreed with the statement 'Trade unions have too much power in this country'. The actives were significantly more likely, however, to agree with the statement on big business and the degree of association was moderately high. The actives and inactives did not differ in the extent to which they agreed/disagreed with the other two statements. Thus overall, the actives tended to have a slightly greater perception of class conflict in society than the inactives, although both groups perceived it to be present to a significant extent.

The steelworkers were also asked two specific questions to determine whether they had a 'teamwork' or 'conflict' image of worker-management relations in society.[14] Rows (iv) and (v) of Table 4.14 give the extent to which the steelworkers agreed or disagreed with the statements 'A firm is like a football team because good teamwork on a side means success and is to everyone's advantage' and 'Teamwork in industry is impossible because employers and men are really on opposite sides'. Row (iv) of the table shows that, while the great majority of both actives and in-actives agreed to some extent with the first statement, the actives were significantly

Table 4.13   Main criteria used to distinguish between social classes for those respondents with communicable images of society
(respondents could give more than one criterion)

| Criteria | (i) All respondents | | (ii) Active respondents | |
	Inactive %	Active %	Type A image %	Other image %
(1) (a) Money, possessions, wages, standard of living as *sole* criteria	16.7 } 76.0	4.8 } 41.9	6.2 } 21.8	3.3 } 53.3
(b) Money, possessions, wages, standard of living in association with other criteria	59.3	37.1	15.6	50.0
(2) Self definition, snobbery, friendliness	1.9	3.2	6.3	0
(3) Behaviour, style of life or dress, area of residence, attitudes	35.2	25.8	31.3	20.0
(4) Background, birth, breeding, education	33.3	37.1	21.9	53.3
(5) Work, job, occupation, position	31.5	24.1	18.8	30.0
(6) Property and business ownership, ability to live on unearned income	24.1	40.3	50.0	30.0
(7) Ability, brains	1.9	4.8	3.1	6.7
(8) Power	0	4.8	9.4	0
	$N=54$	$N=62$	$N=32$	$N=30$

Notes: Column (i) (1) $v.$ (2) to (8) X^2 test P = 0.001, θ = 0.35.
Column (i) (6) $v.$ (1) to (5) and (7) and (8) X^2 test P = 0.10, θ = 0.18.
Column (ii) (1) $v.$ (2) to (8) X^2 test P = 0.05, Ga = 0.21.
Column (ii) (6) $v.$ (1) to (5) and (7) and (8) X^2 test P = 0.10, Ga = 0.20.

Table 4.14   *Respondents' conception of aspects of class conflict and the relationship between management and men in society*

Statement	(1) Strongly agree		(2) Mildly agree		(3) Neither agree nor disagree		(4) Mildly disagree		(5) Strongly disagree		Total	
	Inactive %	Active %	Inactive %	Active %	Inactive %	Active %	Inactive %	Active %	Inactive %	Active %	Inactive %	Active %
(i) 'Big business has too much power in this country'	25.4	47.0	35.6	18.2	22.0	21.2	8.5	9.1	8.5	4.5	100 (N=59)	100 (N=66)
(ii) 'Trade Unions have too much power in this country'	22.0	10.6	27.1	25.8	15.3	13.6	18.6	22.7	16.9	27.3	100 (N=59)	100 (N=66)
(iii) 'There is one law for the rich and one for the poor'	55.9	40.9	20.3	28.8	10.2	6.1	6.8	7.6	6.8	16.7	100 (N=59)	100 (N=66)
(iv) 'A firm is like a football team because good teamwork on a side means success and is to everyone's advantage'	66.1	87.9	5.1	7.6	13.6	1.5	6.8	0	8.5	3.0	100 (N=59)	100 (N=66)
(v) 'Teamwork in industry is impossible because employers and men are really on opposite sides'	15.3	19.7	16.9	10.6	16.9	15.2	32.3	22.7	18.6	31.8	100 (N=59)	100 (N=66)

Notes: Row: (i) X^2 test (1) $v.$ (2) to (5) P = 0.05, G = 0.44.
Row: (ii) X^2 test (4) + (5) $v.$ (1) to (3) P > 0.10
Row: (iii) X^2 test (1) $v.$ (2) to (5) P > 0.10.
Row: (iv) X^2 test (1) $v.$ (2) to (5) P = 0.01, G = 0.57.
Row: (v) X^2 test (5) $v.$ (1) to (4) P > 0.10.

Table 4.15 *Respondents' voting behaviour for the last few elections preceding the interview.*

Vote	Inactive %	Active %
(1) Consistently Labour	66.1	81.8
(2) Consistently Conservative	3.4	0
(3) Changed vote	16.9	7.6
(4) Did not vote	10.2	9.1
(5) Preferred not to answer	0	1.5
(6) Not applicable as respondents were too young to have voted	3.4	0
Total	100	100
	(N=59)	(N=66)

Note: X^2 test (1) v. (2) to (4) P = 0.10, θ = 0.20.

more likely to do so. The degree of association between strongly agreeing with the statement suggesting a harmonious relation and activity was moderately high. However, row (v) shows that a distinctly smaller proportion of both active and inactive steelworkers disagreed with the statement suggesting a conflicting relationship. Similarly, the proportion of the active and inactive groups agreeing with the conflicting statement was larger than the proportions disagreeing with the previous harmonious statement. Also in contrast to the survey results on the first statement, there was no significant difference between actives and inactives here. Perhaps the appropriate conclusion to be drawn from the survey results is that, while a large number of the steelworkers, particularly the actives, appeared to have a positive valuation of the relations between workers and management in society, the fact that they did have some reservations is displayed by their reluctance to disagree strongly with the idea that employers and men might take different sides.[15] This interpretation is considerably strengthened when we remember that the majority of both groups felt that there was some clash of interests between classes in society and that certain elite groups held too much power.

Finally in our discussion of the steelworkers' images of, and opinions on the present-day class structure, the unstructured discussion data were analysed to see how satisfied the steelworkers were and how much change they felt was necessary. Here both groups of members expressed similar views: 41 per cent of the actives and 36 per cent of the inactives considered workers today had their fair share of wealth and income in society, while a somewhat larger proportion of both groups (54 per cent and 59 per cent respectively) felt that the workers' share in society should be improved in some way.[16] However, the respondents tended to see the solution of this problem in terms of redistribution *within* the present social structure rather than through the creation of any new and more 'just' social order. Thus 67 per cent of the dissatisfied actives and 49 per cent of the dissatisfied inactives chose the former solution while 33 per cent of the dissatisfied actives and 49 per cent of the inactives chose the latter.[17]

We will now turn to consider the survey findings on the steelworkers' political attitudes and behaviour. Table 4.15 summarises their choices of political parties in

Table 4.16   *Extent to which respondents discussed*
                politics

Reply choice	Inactive %	Active %
(1) A very great deal	3.4	16.7
(2) Quite a lot	3.4	34.8
(3) Now and then	42.4	27.3
(4) Not very much	35.6	18.2
(5) Not at all	15.3	3.0
Total	100	100
	(N=59)	(N=66)

Note: K − S test P = 0.001, G = 0.64.

the three or four general elections preceding the interview. Here we can see that while the large majority of both groups of members voted consistently for the Labour Party, the actives were suggestively more likely to do so. The degree of association between activity and voting Labour was, however, low. The steelworkers were also asked why they had voted in the last few elections as they had. The survey findings showed no difference here between active and inactive members: the majority of both groups – 80 per cent and 69 per cent respectively – supported the Labour Party on the grounds that it represented the interests of the working class.[18]

The steelworkers were also asked how much they discussed politics and the survey findings displayed here, as can be seen in Table 4.16, a distinct difference between the active and inactive members. Thus the actives were very much more likely to take part in political discussions than were the inactives and the degree of association between activity and discussing politics was relatively high. However, only one active was sufficiently interested in politics to become an individual member of a political party, in this case the Labour Party.[19]

We shall now summarise the survey's findings on the steelworkers' sociopolitical orientations. With regard to image of society, the survey showed that the actives tended to have a dichotomous model of society based on ideological criteria while the inactives tended to have a multi-class image based on material criteria. While both actives and inactives perceived there to be some clash of interests between the various groups in society, the actives were a little more likely to do so. But despite their feelings about class conflict, both actives and inactives had a harmonious team-work image of the relations between men and management in society. However, in contrast to the previous findings, this time the actives were more likely than the inactives to have a non-conflictual image. Both actives and inactives felt that some redistribution of wealth and income should take place within the social structure in the interests of 'social justice'. This ties in closely with the earlier survey finding that actives felt trade unions should work towards this kind of end and not the re-construction of society. On the question of political attitudes and behaviour, the survey showed that while both actives and inactives voted for the Labour Party on the grounds that it represented the working man, the actives were more consistently likely to do so; the actives, as well, were considerably more interested in political affairs.

5

A SURVEY OF THE POSSIBLE SOURCES OF A COMMITMENT TO COLLECTIVISM

Since it has been argued that a certain kind of commitment to collectivism leads to branch participation, either fairly directly or after the operation of some trigger factor, the survey findings now need to be examined to locate the probable sources of this commitment. The survey was on too small a scale to establish any complex causal patterns, but it does provide some strong suggestions. There has, in fact, been little serious discussion of causal factors *per se* in the literature on trade union activism.[1] There have, instead, tended to be rather generalised comments and, in some cases, remarkably silly ones.[2] There has, however, been a much more thorough investigation in Britain of the causal factors associated with political activism which provides a useful guide for identifying relevant factors (see Bochel 1965; Denver and Bochel 1973 and Newton 1969).

The possible causal factors examined in this chapter will be considered under two headings: (1) those factors associated with the socialisation process; and (2) the experience of certain 'significant events'. The section on socialisation adopts (following Brown's (1973) general argument on the sources of orientation to work) an action approach which takes into consideration active and inactive members' past and present work experiences, as well as their past and present social experiences and which also investigates the interaction of the two milieux in the production and sustaining of a commitment to collectivism. The section on events will be concerned with the experience of cataclysmic event/s in a union member's work or out-of-work life which, although not inconsistent with his normal life, yet nevertheless disturbs its equilibrium and has a disproportionate and permanent effect on his subsequent value-system and behaviour. It is also important to adopt a historical perspective in any discussion of, or investigation into, the causal factors associated with a commitment to collectivism and to take into account the impact of events such as the 1930s' depression which, although neither the union member nor his family may personally have experienced them, nevertheless may have an important influence on his views regarding collectivism.

Socialisation

There appear to be two different factors involved in the socialisation process as it concerns commitment to trade unionism: the first is the social class membership of the 'significant others' in the active and inactive members' lives, and the second is the extent to which these 'others' support trade unionism. The general argument here is that the likelihood of union participation is enhanced by social contact with working class and pro-union persons, since this contact encourages the

Table 5.1   *Date of respondents' first joining a trade union*

Date of joining	Inactive %	Active %
1930–39	3.4	13.6
1940–49	11.9	28.8
1950–59	22.0	27.3
1960–69	62.7	30.3
Total	100 (N = 59)	100 (N = 66)

Note: 1-tailed K–S test P = 0.01, G = 0.54

union member to develop a belief in collectivism himself. On the other hand, social contact with middle-class and anti-union persons (or those with no specific views on unionism) diminishes the likelihood of a union member developing the requisite belief and hence his taking part in the union. We shall discuss the survey findings concerning the 'significant others' in the union members' work-related lives first and in their out-of-work lives second. Also included in the first section will be a discussion of how far the steelworkers participated in an 'occupational community' and in the second, the possible influence of the steelworkers' past and present areas of residence. (See Appendix 3 for details of the occupational classification used in the survey.)

Social class and trade union support of the steelworkers' work associates
    The active steelworkers did not differ from the inactive in their prior experience of non-manual work and hence prior contact with non-manual workmates: both groups appear to have only experienced manual work.[3] Thus 57 out of 66 actives (86 per cent) and 51 out of 59 inactives (86 per cent) had never held an intermediate type job and 62 out of 66 actives (94 per cent) and 56 out of 59 inactives (95 per cent) had never held a non-manual job. The actives and the inactives did differ, however, in the length of time they had been trade union members and hence in contact with at least some pro-union workmates. As Table 5.1 shows, the actives were significantly more likely to join at an earlier date than the inactives and we can also note that this relationship held regardless of age; the degree of association was moderately high.
    Turning to the steelworkers' present workmates we find the same pattern. Thus the survey did not show the actives to differ from the inactives in terms of the job status of their 'close workfriends'. Both actives and inactives named exclusively manual workers with only one exception.[4] In contrast, however, the survey showed workmates' opinions on trade unions in general, and these workmates' participation patterns, to be closely related to the respondents' own activity. Columns (iii) to (viii) of Table A3.3 summarise the relevant survey findings. Column (iii) shows that nearly two-thirds of the actives had one or more close workfriends who strongly approved of trade unions, compared to less than a third of the inactives. The difference between the two groups here was suggestive and the degree of association

was moderately high at 0.57. When age was controlled for, important differences were found between younger and older respondents, as can be seen in columns (iv) and (v). The degree of association for the under-40 respondents increased to the high level of 0.73, whereas for those respondents aged 40 and over the relationship was not significant. This difference between the two age groups was due to the high proportion of the younger inactives *not* having a workfriend who strongly approved of trade unions. The proportions of the younger and older actives having at least one such workfriend were similar, being 57 per cent and 65 per cent respectively.

Column (vi) of the same table gives the number of close workfriends each steel-worker had, who undertook a 'great deal' or a 'fair amount' of participation in branch affairs, and shows that over two-thirds of the actives had one or more such friends compared to 39 per cent of the inactives. The difference between the two groups was suggestive and the degree of association was moderately high at 0.55. Again when age was controlled for, considerable differences were found between the younger and older age groups in the relationship between having at least one active workfriend and own activity, as can be seen from columns (vii) and (viii). The degree of association between the two variables for the respondents aged under 40 rose to 0.85 (one of the highest in the survey) while the relationship between the two variables was not significant for those respondents aged 40 and over. The proportion of younger active respondents having at least one active workfriend was 86 per cent and that for the older actives was 56 per cent. Thus the younger active respondents were not only much more likely than their inactive counterparts to have work friends favourable towards trade unions, they were also much more likely to have fellow actives as workfriends and it is likely that this affected in some way the development of their commitment to collectivism. However, both younger *and* older actives were likely to have been in contact with pro-trade union persons for longer periods than their inactive counterparts through their having been trade union members for a significantly longer time as we saw above.

One work-related feature of socialisation, which has been shown to have important consequences for the development of a commitment to unionism amongst union members in certain industries, is the extent to which union members participate in the occupational community. There have been many studies of the occupational cultures and communities formed by workers such as printers, dockers, miners, fishermen, railwaymen and textile workers, and workers in these industries have been described as having strong beliefs in collectivism and high levels of participation (in some form or other) in the union.[5] More specifically, Lipset *et al.*'s (1956, pp. 72–5, 83–92) work on printers has shown participation in the occupational community to be significantly linked to participation in the union.[6]

A number of measures of participation in an occupational community was used in the survey to look at this suggestion: number of fellow workers seen outside of work and preferential association with other steelworkers; amount of talking about work outside of work; and participation in work-based associations. We have already seen in Chapter 3 that while the actives were a little more likely than the inactives – although not significantly or suggestively so – to see close workfriends outside of work, the numbers of workmates seen was not great for either group. With regard to preferential association with other steelworkers the survey showed that the actives were suggestively more likely than the inactives to have spare-time companions also employed in the steel industry, as column (iv) of Table A3.6 shows. Nearly three-quarters of the actives had at least one companion who was a steelworker compared to 60 per cent of the inactives. However, the degree of association between activity and having such companions was low at 0.24 and few actives had more than two such companions. Furthermore, this relationship was mainly due to the fact that actives tended, as column (v) of the same table shows, more so than the inactives, to name workmates as their spare time companions; thus, in effect, merely echoing the previous survey finding on seeing workfriends outside of work. Again work was not found to be a perennial topic of conversation among the actives or the inactives; roughly 60 per cent of both actives and inactives (40 out of 66 and 36 out of 59 respectively), when asked how much they discussed work with their family and friends outside of work, chose the replies 'not very much' or 'not at all'.

Final confirmation that work did not play an important part in the active and inactive respondents' out-of-work life was provided by the survey's findings on the two groups' membership of and participation in the BSC's work-based clubs. While the numbers of both active and inactive respondents belonging either to the social club or one of the sport clubs was moderately high – 45 out of 66 actives and 32 out of 59 inactives – very few took an active part in these: in fact none of the inactives and only seven of the actives did so.

Thus it appears that neither the actives nor the inactives participated to any significant extent in an occupational community. The fact that the actives saw a little more of their workmates outside of work is more convincingly interpreted, in light of the steelworkers' tendency not to talk about their work in their out-of-work lives and not to take part in work-based activities, as an outcome of the actives' greater sociability tendencies noted in Chapter 3. Consequently it seems unlikely that the actives derived their commitment to collectivism through participation in an occupational community.

Social class and trade union support of the steelworkers' out-of-work associates

With regard to the social class of the steelworkers' families of origin and marriage, the survey found no significant differences between the active and inactive respondents. The survey findings here are summarised in Tables A3.2, A3.7, A3.8 and A3.9. We can see that few of the active or inactive steelworkers had fathers, siblings or adult children with intermediate or non-manual occupations, and less than half of the actives and inactives had wives with past or present intermediate or non-manual occupations. With regard to the extent of trade union support among the steelworkers' kin, the survey findings, in contrast, found considerable differences between the actives and inactives. Although the kin members' membership of a trade union was relatively unimportant, their opinions on trade unions and their own activity patterns were very important. The survey findings are again summarised in Tables A3.2, A3.7, A3.8 and A3.9.

Table A3.8 shows that while father's trade union membership was not related to the steelworkers' activity – the majority of both actives' and inactives' fathers belonged – the degree of association between the steelworkers' activity and having a father who approved of trade unions was moderately high at 0.40 and between it and having a father who himself participated in a branch was a little higher at 0.45. Thus 48 per cent of the actives compared to 29 per cent of the inactives had a father who 'strongly approved' of trade unions and 42 per cent of the actives compared to 21 per cent of the inactives had a father who participated in branch affairs a 'great deal' or a 'fair amount'.

Table A3.7 shows again that, while the extent to which the steelworkers' siblings belonged to trade unions was not important, the degree of association between a steelworker's activity and number of siblings who 'strongly approved' of trade unions was moderate at 0.43 and that between activity and number of siblings who undertook a 'great deal' or a 'fair amount' of branch activity was 0.57, a relatively high figure. Thus 58 per cent of the actives compared to 29 per cent of the inactives had one or more siblings who 'strongly approved' of trade unions and 46 per cent of the actives compared to 17 per cent of the inactives had one or more siblings who undertook a 'great deal' or a 'fair amount' of branch activity.

As might be expected, the general levels of trade union membership, approval and activity were lower in the case of the respondents' wives, but there were still important differences here between the actives and inactives as can be seen in Table A3.9. The actives were suggestively more likely to have a wife who belonged at some time to a trade union although the degree of association was moderately low at 0.30. However, the degrees of association between the respondents' activity and having a wife who approved of trade unions was moderately high at 0.57 and that between the respondents' activity and having a wife who participated in branch affairs was higher still at 0.62. Thus 46 per cent of the actives compared to 22 per cent of the inactives had wives who 'strongly approved' or 'mildly approved' of trade unions and 39 per cent of actives compared to only 13 per cent of the inactives had wives who participated in branch affairs a 'great deal', a 'fair amount' or a 'little'.

This pattern continues when we come to examine the trade union characteristics of those of the steelworkers' children who were old enough to have left school and be at work themselves, as can be seen in Table A3.2. While childrens' trade union membership was not significantly related to their fathers' activity, these childrens' attitudes to trade unions and their participation in branch affairs very definitely were (despite in the latter case the very small number of children involved): the degrees of association being 0.81 and 0.85 respectively. Forty-eight per cent of the actives with adult children, compared to only 9 per cent of the inactives, had at least one adult child who strongly approved of trade unions, and 50 per cent of the actives with adult children had an adult child who participated in branch activity a 'great deal', a 'fair amount' or a 'little', whereas only one (8 per cent) of the inactives did.

Thus the survey findings show the branch activity patterns, and particularly the attitudes on trade unions, of kin members to be strongly related to the steelworkers' own activity, suggesting that kin influence is an important factor in building up commitment, and this was so regardless of age. Many of the actives themselves stressed the importance of the role of the views and behaviour of members of their families in the development of their own views during the open-ended discussions held at the end of the interview. One final interesting point to note here is that the 66 actives between them had 30 kin members holding trade union official positions, whereas the 59 inactives had only 11 such kin members. The quotes overleaf illustrate the importance of family influence in the development of a commitment to collectivism:

Me father, me grandfather, especially me grandfather, told me a lot about trade unions. He always used to tell me that if I ever went into the steelworks to make sure I was always up to date (with union subscription) because while ever you were member of union, big gaffers couldn't knock you about or mess you about as much as others.

My father used to always believe in trade unions and he dug it into me and although I believed in unions I weren't prepared to be active and give my time up, this was the reason and more or less once I did start and gradually get more and more involved and automatically I suppose I, although I had a basic belief, I started to put it into practice when I got on.

My father used to take me (to trade union meetings) when I was old enough to go and then we used to have a bit of jollification after meeting were closed, you know, companionship and drinking and what have you . . . he put me wise about trade unions.

We turn next to the influence of the steelworkers' leisure-time companions. While there were no important differences between the actives and inactives in the number of companions with intermediate or non-manual occupations they possessed or in the proportion of their companions who belonged to a trade union, there were large differences between the two groups in terms of their companions' attitudes towards trade unions and their branch participation patterns as can be seen in Table A3.6. The degrees of association here between activity and having companions 'strongly approving' of trade unions, and between it and having companions who participated in branch affairs, were 0.62 in the first case and, in the second, higher at 0.81. Thus 70 per cent of the actives, compared to 32 per cent of the inactives, had one or more companions who 'strongly approved' of trade unions and 58 per cent of the actives, compared to only 14 per cent of the inactives, had one or more companions who undertook a 'great deal' or a 'fair amount' of branch activity.

When age was controlled for, however, important differences were found between the two age groups in terms of the relationship between companions' trade union attitudes and activity, and the respondents' own activity. For the younger active and inactive respondents, the degree of association between having at least one companion who strongly approved of trade unionism and activity increased to the very high level indeed of 0.94, while on the other hand the relationship between the two variables was suggestive for the older actives, with a degree of association of 0.39, as can be seen in columns (vii) and (viii) of Table A3.6. Thus 85 per cent of the younger actives had at least one companion who strongly approved compared to 61 per cent of the older actives. The age breakdown for companions' trade union activity displayed a similar pattern, as can be seen in columns (xi) and (xii) of the same table. The degree of association between having at least one companion who participated a 'great deal' or a 'fair amount' in branch affairs and the respondent's own activity increased for the younger actives to 0.87, while the degree of association for the older respondents decreased slightly to 0.76. Thus 70 per cent of the younger actives compared to 48 per cent of the older actives had at least one companion who was active in branch affairs.

Thus the survey findings show the attitudes towards trade unionism and patterns of branch participation of the actives' leisure time companions to be remarkably

60

similar to their own, particularly in the case of the younger actives. The possibility must therefore be considered that their companions' influence played some role in the development of the actives' commitment to collectivism.

Having looked at the social and trade union characteristics of the 'significant others' in the steelworkers' out-of-work lives, we turn now to consider the possibility that the type of area or neighbourhood in which the actives now live, or that in which they grew up, influenced the development of their commitment to collectivism: i.e. certain neighbourhoods are more likely to contain working-class and pro-union inhabitants than others. Little or no attention has been paid to the character of the specific neighbourhood union members live/grew up in in determining the causal factors involved in participation. Writers in this area have tended (Tannenbaum and Kahn 1958, pp. 112–5; Whyte 1944) to concentrate on the one hand, on the wider question of the rural/urban origin of active and inactive members (which is of small significance for the UK) or, on the other, on general descriptions of the one-class, isolated and hence strongly pro-union communities associated with industries such as coal-mining and docking, which must be treated as a special case (Dennis *et al.* 1956; *The Dockworker*; Seidman *et al.* 1958, Chapter 2). However, only a minority of active trade unionists in the UK would reside in such communities, and these communities are in any case said to be rapidly disappearing features of British industrial society, with the decline of traditional industries and with the increase of voluntary or involuntary residential mobility of their inhabitants (Lockwood 1966, pp. 254–5).

The kind of enumeration district (as defined in the Introduction to Appendix 3) in which the steelworkers in the survey live at present is shown in column (i) of Table A3.10. Here we can see that there were no significant differences between the actives and inactives; roughly half of both groups (53 per cent and 49 per cent respectively) lived in districts dominated by council housing. Most of the rest of the active and inactive respondents lived either in districts where most residents rented their homes and where there was a large element of semi-skilled and unskilled workers (20 per cent and 17 per cent respectively), or in districts where most residents owned their own houses but did not have predominantly professional or semi-professional occupations (14 per cent and 24 per cent respectively).[7]

The survey findings also showed that nearly all of the enumeration districts lived in by the respondents were situated in urban areas: only five out of 66 actives and three out of 59 inactives lived in rural enumeration districts and nearly all of these lived in what had once been mining villages. In addition, the respondents tended to live in enumeration districts on the outskirts of the Sheffield/Rotherham conurbation, rather than in those situated near either of the city centres or in those near to the industrial areas; in particular few respondents – only six actives and five inactives – lived in any of the enumeration districts surrounding the steel works.[8]

Turning to the question of the respondents' own homes, no significant differences were found between the actives and inactives in their type of tenure.[9] About half of all the steelworkers in the samples, as would be expected, lived in council houses themselves – 32 out of 66 actives and 32 out of 59 inactives. These council houses were mainly semi-detached and built either just before the second world war or in the post-war period; the median number of years the respondents had lived in their present homes for this category of tenure was six years.[10]

About a third of both groups – 26 out of 66 actives and 20 out of 59 inactives – had bought, or were in the process of buying, their own homes. These steelworkers tended to buy homes in areas which, though dominated by owner occupiers, did not have a large element of professional or semi-professional persons living there.[11] These houses again tended to be semi-detached and built in the period just before or after the war; these steelworkers had bought them on average (median) seven years before.[12] Only a small proportion of the actives and inactives lived in privately-rented accommodation – 8 out of 66 actives and 7 out of 59 inactives. These respondents lived mainly in terraced houses built at the turn of the century; the amount of time they had lived in their present homes was extremely varied, ranging from two to 57 years.[13]

Column (ii) of Table A3.10 shows the type of districts in which the active and inactive steelworkers grew up. We can see that although the active and inactives both tended to have been brought up in a 'rented rough' type urban area, the actives were suggestively more likely to than the inactives (52 per cent as compared to 33 per cent). Many of the actives described areas that we would currently label as 'slums' and indeed they themselves frequently referred to them as such. The degree of association between being brought up in a 'rented rough' type area and branch activity was small at 0.19. But when age was controlled for, it was found, as columns (iii) and (iv) of Table A3.10 show, that the degree of association between being brought up in a 'rented rough' urban area and union activity did increase for the older respondents to 0.26 while the relationship between the two variables was not significant for the younger respondents.

Thus the survey findings do not suggest that the actives lived in a different type of neighbourhood from that of the inactives: both groups lived predominantly on attractive council estates, or in the case of about a third on low-cost privately developed ones, on the outskirts of the Sheffield/Rotherham conurbation, estates which in both cases contained a mixture of manual, intermediate and white-collar workers. In contrast, however, to their present comfortable circumstances, many of the older steelworkers, and in particular the older actives, had spent their childhoods in slums or near slums.

The role of 'significant events'

The experience of cataclysmic events such as unemployment and/or poverty, which disturb union members' lives and permanently affect their subsequent value-systems and behaviour, has not been very thoroughly investigated before. Not mentioned at all in the literature on trade union activism (or political activism for that matter), but which I also considered essential to be included in this study of blue-collar activism, is experience of striking, both for union members themselves and for their fathers. In particular, I considered that experience of the 1926 General Strike (either at first hand or at second hand through a father's experience) should be investigated.

The survey findings for the steelworkers' own experiences of unemployment and striking, and those of their fathers, are summarised in Table 5.2. Here we can see from column (i) that few of the actives or inactives had any experience of unemployment, and for those who had, the experience was relatively minor. However, column (ii) of the table shows that the active and inactive respondents did differ significantly in their experience of striking: whereas over half of the actives had strike experience

Table 5.2 *Respondents' personal experiences of unemployment and striking and those of their fathers*

Extent of experience	(i) Respondents' unemployment experience[a]		(ii) Respondents' strike experience[b] All respondents		(iii) Respondents aged under 40 years		(iv) Respondents aged 40 years or more		(v) Unemployment experience of respondents' fathers[c] All respondents		(vi) Respondents aged under 40 years		(vii) Respondents aged 40 years or more		(viii) Strike experience of respondents' fathers[d] All respondents		(ix) Respondents aged under 40 years		(x) Respondents aged 40 years or more	
	Inactive %	Active %	Inactive %	Active %	Inactive %	Active %	Inactive %	Active %	Inactive %	Active %	Inactive %	Active %	Inactive %	Active %	Inactive %	Active %	Inactive %	Active %	Inactive %	Active %
(1) Major	0	0	3.4	13.6	6.5	8.3	0	16.7	25.4	45.5	19.4	25.0	32.1	57.1	11.9	27.3	9.7	12.5	14.3	35.7
(2) Minor	10.2	15.2	23.7	37.9	22.6	33.3	25.0	40.5	10.2	4.5	3.2	0	17.9	7.1	6.8	6.1	3.2	8.3	10.7	4.8
(3) None	89.8	84.8	72.9	48.5	71.0	58.3	75.0	42.9	57.6	50.0	67.7	75.0	46.4	35.7	76.3	65.2	77.4	75.0	75.0	59.5
(4) Can't remember /don't know	N/A	N/A	N/A	N/A	N/A	N/A	N/A	N/A	6.8	0	9.7	0	3.6	0	5.1	1.5	9.7	4.2	0	0
Total	100 (N=59)	100 (N=66)	100 (N=59)	100 (N=66)	100 (N=31)	100 (N=24)	100 (N=28)	100 (N=42)	100 (N=59)	100 (N=66)	100 (N=31)	100 (N=24)	100 (N=28)	100 (N=42)	100 (N=59)	100 (N=66)	100 (N=31)	100 (N=24)	100 (N=28)	100 (N=42)

Notes:
Column (ii)   1-tailed X^2 test (1) + (2) *v.* (3) P = 0.01, G = 0.48.
Column (iii) 1-tailed X^2 test (1) + (2) *v.* (3) P > 0.10,
Column (iv)   1-tailed X^2 test (1) + (2) *v.* (3) P = 0.05, G = 0.63.
Column (v)   1-tailed X^2 test (1) *v.* (2) to (4) P = 0.05, G = 0.28.
Column (vi)   1-tailed X^2 test (1) *v.* (2) to (4) P > 0.10.
Column (vii) 1-tailed X^2 test (1) *v.* (2) to (4) P = 0.05, G = 0.56.
Column (viii) 1-tailed X^2 test (1) *v.* (2) to (4) P = 0.05, G = 0.36.
Column (ix)   1-tailed X^2 test (1) *v.* (2) to (4) P > 0.10.
Column (x)   1-tailed X^2 test (1) *v.* (2) to (4) P = 0.05, G = 0.37.

[a] The respondent was asked if he had ever been unemployed for a period longer than a month. If he replied that he had, he was asked how many times, how long each unemployment period had lasted and what he remembered about each occasion. His replies were coded on the basis of his answers to all four questions into one of the three categories of experience in the table.

[b] The respondent was asked here whether he had ever been on strike. If he replied that he had, he was further asked how many times, how long each strike had lasted and what he remembered about each occasion. His replies were coded as above.

[c] The respondent was asked whether he remembered his father ever being unemployed or on 'short time'. If he replied that he did, he was asked to give an account of what he remembered and how it affected his family. His replies were classified into one of the four categories in the table.

[d] The respondent was asked whether he remembered his father ever being on strike. If he replied that he did, he was asked to give an account of what he remembered and how it had affected his family. His account was classified as above.

of some kind, nearly three-quarters of the inactives had never been on one. The degree of association here was moderate. However, when age was controlled for, it was apparent as columns (iii) and (iv) show, that whereas the significant relationship between striking experience and activity disappeared for the under-40s, the degree of association for the two variables increased for the 40 and over group to a relatively high value. Thus 57 per cent of the older actives had strike experience of some kind compared to 42 per cent of the younger actives.

Column (v) of Table 5.2 shows that the actives were significantly more likely than the inactives to remember their father having had one or more major experiences of unemployment: nearly half of the actives had a father with such experience compared to only a quarter of the inactives. The degree of association here between the two variables was low. But when age was controlled for, important differences were found between the sub-groups, as can be seen in columns (vi) and (vii). The degree of association increased for the respondents aged 40 and over, whereas the relationship between the two variables was not significant for those aged under 40. Thus 57 per cent of the older actives remembered their father having a major experience of unemployment compared to a quarter of the younger actives: many of these older actives referred to the early 1930s when the unemployment rate in Sheffield was particularly high.

The last three columns of Table 5.2 give the breakdown of their fathers' strike experience as remembered by the steel workers. Column (viii) shows that the actives were significantly more likely to remember their fathers having been on one or more major strikes than were the inactives. The degree of association between such remembrance and activity was moderate. But when age was controlled for, the pattern previously found in the case of respondents' own strike experience was repeated, as can be seen in columns (ix) and (x). The relationship between remembering their father having been out on a major strike and activity disappeared for the younger group, whereas the degree of association between the two variables slightly increased for the older group; many of the respondents referred to their fathers' coming out in the General Strike of 1926. Indeed very few of the younger respondents, active or inactive, remembered their fathers' having been on any strike.

In addition we should note that the findings on the strike experience of respondents' fathers are very similar to those we found previously on their fathers' unemployment experience. One further survey finding which combined elements from the respondents' accounts, both of their fathers' strike experience and of their fathers' unemployment or short time experience, shows a higher degree of association than was found for the two variables separately. For this, each respondent's account was sub-coded for the specific mention of 'hard times' experienced by his family in his childhood, when his father was unemployed or on strike. Column (i) of Table 5.3 shows the number of respondents who mentioned that their families had experienced 'hard times' compared to those who did not, because their fathers had not been unemployed or on strike for any substantial period of time. Here we can see that more than twice as many actives as inactives mentioned the 'hard times' experienced by their families and the degree of association was relatively high. When age was controlled for, the degree of association, as would be expected, increased for the 40 and over group, whereas the relationship between the two variables was not significant for the under-40 group, as can be seen in columns (ii) and (iii) of the table. Memories

64

Table 5.3   *Specific mention of 'hard times' experienced by respondents' families when their fathers were unemployed or on strike*

	(i)		(ii)		(iii)	
	All respondents		Respondents aged under 40 years		Respondents aged 40 years or more	
	Inactive %	Active %	Inactive %	Active %	Inactive %	Active %
'Hard times' mentioned	23.7	57.6	16.1	29.2	32.1	73.8
No mention	76.3	42.4	83.9	70.8	67.9	26.2
Total	100	100	100	100	100	100
	(N=59)	(N=66)	(N=31)	(N=24)	(N=28)	(N=42)

Notes:
Column (i) X^2 test P = 0.001, G = 0.63.
Column (ii) X^2 test P > 0.10.
Column (iii) X^2 test P = 0.01, G = 0.71.

of these 'hard times' were often very vivid and had obviously left a deep and lasting impression on many actives as the comments below show:

> He (father) was on 1926 miners' strike, 1933 to 1936 he was unemployed. . .
> I were seven years old then. . .we used to go and pick the scrap coal off the slag tips. I don't know how we used to manage. There was the allotment and how we got the stuff to sow, I don't know. . . . . .went to school with no shoes on. . . .I remember I was eleven before I went to the sea-side on a day trip, I'd never seen the sea before. My little girl, she'd be only about ten, and she's seen more than I ever saw in my early life.

> Things were very, very bad (when father was out on the 1926 General Strike), there were eight of us going to school. We used to go out-cropping for coal and, you know, earn a copper here and there when you could.

> I remember going to school in clogs and having bread and dripping for every ruddy meal. A family of ten and only one working at that time, things were tight. (Father unemployed just after the second world war.)

It was also possible to utilise here additional information on the steelworkers' personal experience of job grievances which was collected in the course of determining the steelworkers' attitudes towards taking up grievances (see Chapter 3). This information is presented in Table 5.4. Column (1) shows that the actives were significantly more likely than the inactives to have had experience of a job grievance and the degree of association between the two variables was moderately high. When age was controlled for, the same pattern appeared as was found above in the case of respondents' personal strike experience and the experiences of adversity of their fathers. Thus the degree of association between activity and experience of job grievance increased to a relatively high figure for the older steelworkers, while the relationship was not significant for the younger steelworkers, as can be seen in columns (ii) and (iii).

Table 5.4   *Respondents' experiences of personal job grievances*

	(i)		(ii)		(iii)	
	All respondents		Respondents aged under 40 years		Respondents aged 40 years or more	
	Inactive %	Active %	Inactive %	Active %	Inactive %	Active %
Never had a personal grievance	57.6	25.8	45.2	25.0	71.4	26.2
Had a personal job grievance at some time	42.4	74.2	54.8	75.0	28.6	73.8
Total	100 (*N*=59)	100 (*N*=66)	100 (*N*=31)	100 (*N*=24)	100 (*N*=28)	100 (*N*=42)

Notes:
Column (i) X^2 test P = 0.001, G = 0.59.
Column (ii) X^2 test P > 0.10.
Column (iii) X^2 test P = 0.001, G = 0.75.

Thus overall in this section, the survey findings showed that the older active respondents had, in comparison to their inactive counterparts significantly more experience of adverse events: not only of being on strike themselves and of personal job grievances but also of adverse experiences at second hand through their fathers being on strike or being unemployed for substantial lengths of time, and thus being considerably more likely to remember experiences of 'hard times' from their childhood. However, personal experience of unemployment did not distinguish between the older actives and inactives. Neither the younger actives or inactives, on the other hand, appeared to have had any significant experience of striking or unemployment, either at first hand or through their fathers.

We shall now attempt to draw some conclusions on the factors that appear to be associated in this study of steelworkers with the development of a commitment to collectivism. In the context of socialisation, the survey shows that neither actives nor inactives were involved to any significant extent in an occupational community: while many of the respondents did number a steel worker among their associates, this is hardly surprising considering they were living in an area dominated by the steel industry. Thus it seems unlikely that the actives in the survey derived their commitment to collectivism from greater participation in an occupational community. The actives also seemed unlikely to have derived their commitment to collectivism from living in a different type of neighbourhood from the inactives. Indeed, both groups had similar life-styles, the majority living in attractive, relatively modern council estates.

The social class membership of the steelworkers' associates did not appear to be an important factor in the development of a commitment to collectivism. Both active and inactive groups had working class workfriends, fathers, siblings and adult children, and about half of both groups had wives with past or present intermediate or non-manual occupations. Again trade union membership did not appear in general to be an important factor. The majority of both active and inactive groups had fathers and at least one sibling who was a member, and a third of both groups had wives or adult children who were members.

The important differences between actives and inactives in the context of social-isation were their associates' attitudes to trade unionism and for those associates who were trade union members, the extent of their participation in branch affairs. Both older and younger actives were much more likely than their inactive counter-parts to have pro-union and active fathers, siblings, wives and adult children. The degrees of association found in the survey between kin's trade union characteristics and activity ranged from moderate to, in the case of the adult children's character-istics, relatively high. In all cases, the degree of association was higher between the respondents' activity patterns and those of their kin than it was between the respondents' activity patterns and the trade union attitude of their kin. The younger actives, however, were also a great deal more likely than their inactive counterparts to have pro-union and active workfriends as well as kin, while the older actives were not. In addition, the younger actives were a great deal more likely than their inactive counterparts to have pro-union leisure-time companions: while the older actives were significantly more likely to than their inactive counterparts, the difference was not so marked. However, both younger and older actives were a great deal more likely to have companions active in branch affairs. The degrees of association found between the activity patterns of the younger respondents and the attitudes and activities of their workfriends and leisure-time companions were among the highest found in the survey.

Since so few of the actives, older or younger, directly referred to the influence of their associates in first joining a union, in first becoming active in a branch and for continuing to be active in their present branch, it seems clear that being sur-rounded by pro-union and active people does not itself lead directly to participation, but rather plays some kind of role in the development of a person's commitment to trade unionism: it is this commitment which, when fully developed, leads to par-ticipation, either directly or as a result of being stimulated by the occurrence of some incident. It is being argued here, for reasons which will shortly be given, that the relationship between the pro-trade union attitudes and activity of the actives' families or origin, workfriends and leisure-time companions, and the actives' com-mitment, is causal. It also seems reasonable to argue that the pro-trade-union attitudes and characteristics of the actives' families of marriage do not have a causal role, but that having a pro-trade-union wife reinforces an active's commitment, perhaps mak-ing it easier for him both to become and to remain active, and that the trade union characteristics of his children show how the pattern is repeated from generation to generation.

The adverse experiences undergone by the older actives, mostly in the inter-war years or just after the second world war, can be readily seen to play a causal role in the development of the older actives' commitment to trade unionism, especially since some of them are likely to have occurred during the actives' childhood. These experiences, as related by the older actives, do indeed appear to have had a dramatic and permanent effect on their subsequent value-systems and behaviour. The survey findings here underline the importance of the historical perspective in studies of this kind. The younger actives had little opportunity of experiencing such adverse events. However, one line of research that it might be profitable to pursue in future research with respect to the socialisation process, is whether younger actives had heard family accounts of the deprivation and hardships in 1926 or in the 1930s suffered by their grandfathers or other family members of the same generation. The influence of accounts of hard times in the past, transmitted through the media, could also be considered.[14]

When the survey findings on the steelworkers' experiences of socialisation and cataclysmic events are combined, we find that, overall, the older and younger actives appear to have acquired their commitment to trade unionism in different ways. The older actives differed from their inactive counterparts mainly in terms of their greater experience of certain events, while, for the younger actives, a greater association with particular people seemed to be the important factor. Thus the older actives were much more likely than their inactive counterparts to have, or have had, a father with experience of striking and unemployment, to come from a family which had experienced hard times on this account, and to have lived in a slum or near slum as a child. What is also important is that the older actives underwent these experiences of adversity in the context of a pro-union family of origin. Furthermore, the older actives had had, compared to the older inactives, more experiences of being on strike themselves and of personal job grievances: the fact that the older actives tended to have pro-union and active companions suggests that they might have undergone their own experiences of adversity similarly in a pro-union context. While the younger actives had no such experiences of adversity, what *was* compelling in the survey's findings was the way in which these younger members were surrounded by associates who were both pro-union and active themselves. The younger actives not only had more pro-union and active kin than their inactive counterparts, but they also had a great many more leisure-time companions and workfriends with similar characteristics.

The exact meaning in causal terms of the relationship between the younger actives' commitment and the trade union attitudes and activities of their associates is difficult to establish and a survey with much greater resources would be needed to investigate it. In fact the relationship established between such younger actives' association and activity could reasonably be interpreted in several ways: that association with pro-union and active persons leads directly to a respondent's becoming active; that the active selects pro-union and active friends from his environment, either for congruence with his own views or because he so frequently comes into contact with such people through his own activity; or that the active's beliefs in trade-unionism – which lead him to become active – are reinforced by his contact with pro-union and active associates which, in turn, leads him to participate more. I argue here that the influence of the younger actives' associates is at least to some extent causal since: (i) the decrease in importance of experiences of adversity for the younger actives, and the increase in their number of pro-union and active associates, suggests that these two types of factors are *counterbalancing* each other; and (ii) neither the younger nor the older actives' *families of marriage* had had harsh experiences, when the chief breadwinner – i.e. the active himself – was unemployed or on strike for a considerable period of time, in any way comparable to the experiences of families in the 1930s and 1926, and yet the actives' children who were old enough to be at work were pro-union and – if they belonged to a trade union – were active as well. This adds weight to the idea that pro-union sympathies and a predisposition for participation can be transmitted from generation to generation and that personal experience of harsh events is not a necessary requisite for the development of a commitment to trade unionism. It also follows that if union sympathies can be transmitted from parents to children, so can they be from workfriends and leisure time companions.

6

A MODEL OF BLUE-COLLAR BRANCH
PARTICIPATION

This chapter attempts to relate systematically the survey findings to the various theories set out in Chapter 1, and considers the possibility of a new theory to explain local participation in trade unions, beginning with the most consistently expounded theory, that of the 'stake-in-the-job'.

There was some positive support for the 'stake-in-the-job' theory from the survey findings that activity was related to skill and marital status, and to a very limited extent with job satisfaction, including the tendency to make friends at work. For the younger actives alone, there was also some support for the contentions on seniority and number of dependent children.

However, there was no support for the other predictions of this theory. In particular, there was no support at all for its major propositions on the actives' view of trade unions' functions and on their motivation for becoming and continuing to be active. The actives did not participate in branch unionism to protect and enhance the interests and rights of their particular jobs, nor did they see this to be the main function of trade unionism. There was also no support for this theory's key predictions that activity was correlated with age and attitude to management. Nor finally was there any relationship between activity and the composite variables of 'dual allegiance' and 'social integration'.

There are also alternative explanations for some of the survey's positive findings. The relationship of activity and skill in particular, as we shall see later, is capable of alternative interpretation. Making friends at work can be seen as an indication of sociability rather than job satisfaction, and a high opinion of the branch's performance can perhaps be more readily seen as a concomitant of participation rather than as a cause.

Thus it is quite clear that the 'stake-in-the-job' theory does not provide an adequate explanation for the participation in the two branches of BISAKTA in the Sheffield/Rotherham area covered by the survey. There is also little evidence from the survey findings to support the contentions of authors, such as Kyllonen, Gouldner, and Galenson, that actives participate in order to gain other kinds of individual ends extrinsic to the trade union movement, such as the satisfaction of pecuniary, social and psychological needs, or promotion within the union or within the firm. The actives themselves did not refer to the satisfaction of such needs in their own explanations of their activity and, while it is acknowledged that they might be unlikely to admit to some of these motives in an interview, it can be pointed out that only a very small proportion of the inactives accused the actives of participating in the branch in order to gain these ends. The survey also provided conclusive empirical evidence that the actives did not lack a complete family-children-kin pattern, contrary to Kyllonen's contention. Again the actives did not refer to their hopes for becoming full-time union officials or foremen when accounting for their participation. There is the additional evidence from the survey that few of the actives in fact wanted to be foremen; and while about a quarter of the actives replied that they would like to become a full-time union official, it is possible, as noted previously, that the design of the survey question led to some exaggeration of the extent of the actives' ambitions here.

Nor, on the other hand, did the survey findings support the 'political agitator' theory, that the active seeks to use the union to gain radical political ends extrinsic to the trade union movement for the group he identifies with. None of the actives belonged to the Communist Party or any other radical political party; and while one active said he would have voted for the Communist Party in the three or four General Elections preceding the interview had there been a candidate in his constituency (and actually voted Labour as the only alternative), none of the other actives indicated any interest whatsoever in radical politics. Furthermore, the actives' views on the functions of trade unionism, the structure of present-day society and hopes for future social development were not consistent with a commitment to a radical political ideology.

The 'technological implications' approach can also be fairly quickly dismissed. The survey findings on job accessibility and the clustering of activity by rota and department did not in general support the contentions of this hypothesis. Furthermore, very few actives gave technological reasons or referred to the development of mutual interest amongst persons on their rota in their department, in either their accounts of first becoming active or in their reasons for continuing to be active. Thus this hypothesis is not only theoretically limited, as seen in Chapter 1, but it is also not afforded any empirical support by the survey findings. We must therefore continue our search for a viable theory.

We consequently turn to an examination of the 'social activity' theme, which suggests that the actives are more outgoing, ascendent and social than the inactives and that participation in the union is one of the outlets for their social drive and a source of social rewards. Apart from the contention that the actives participate more in non-union formal organisations – which had a reasonable level of support from the survey findings – the degrees of association between activity and the various other measures of sociability were on the low side. Again, while roughly a quarter of the actives stressed their enjoyment in 'knowing what's going off' in giving the reasons for taking part in their present branch, and while the actives were more likely than the inactives to believe trade unions should provide a social milieux for their members, yet few or no actives referred to their social drive in giving their reasons for first joining a trade union or in the accounts they gave of how they first became active in a branch. Furthermore, political and especially economic, goals clearly superseded social goals in actives' ordering of trade union priorities. In addition it should be noted that there are alternative explanations for the correlation between trade union activity and participation in other formal organisations, as shall be seen later.

Having reviewed the weaknesses of the above theories in explaining the survey findings, it is now possible to attempt to develop a new model of branch activism

71

based on the study of active and inactive members of the two branches of BISAKTA in the Sheffield/Rotherham area. This model will be presented as a series of conclusions and the various survey findings from Chapters 4 and 5 supporting each conclusion will be enumerated. Then what evidence there is in the general body of industrial and political sociology lending support to these conclusions will be considered.

CONCLUSION 1 states that: *the active steelworkers in the study were clearly motivated to participate in their branch of BISAKTA by a belief in, and a commitment to, the value of collectivism – the group pursuit of group goals: a commitment that was not shared by the inactive steelworkers.*

This conclusion can be derived from the following survey findings:

(i)   that a belief in collectivism played by far the most part in the reasons given by the actives to account for their first joining a trade union, for their first becoming active in a branch, and for their continuing to be active in their present branch;

(ii)   that the inactives referred significantly more frequently than the actives to their individual benefit in describing how they first came to join a trade union, that the inactives explained their low level of participation as the outcome of their lack of any deep interest in trade unionism, and that the inactives saw actives as being motivated by the kind of interest and belief they themselves lacked;

(iii)   that the actives were much more willing than the inactives to use collective action in the form of striking;

(iv)   (from Chapter 3) that the actives were much more willing than the inactives to use collective machinery for processing their individual job grievances.

The notion that is clear in, or certainly implicit in, much of the general literature on trade unions in both Western Europe and the USA, that workers do hold beliefs in trade unionism as a collective movement, whatever they may feel its particular aims to be, supports this conclusion. This explicit, or implicit, interpretation ranges in Great Britain from the Webbs' writings (1902, pp. 431–8), through the 1950s' classical studies of trade unionism such as Dennis *et al.*'s *Coal is Our Life* and the University of Liverpool's *The Dockworker*, to modern studies such as Goldthorpe *et al.*'s *The Affluent Worker* or Beynon's *Working for Ford*. It includes other West European studies such as those by Popitz *et al.* (1969) on steel workers in West Germany and Durand's (1971B) work on a cross section of workers in France. Even in the USA, the home of the 'stake-in-the-job' theory, this interpretation is manifest in the work on occupational groups such as miners, plumbers and steel workers of Joel Seidman and his colleagues (1958) at Chicago and in Lipset *et al.*'s (1956) work on printers.

Having shown that the active members were motivated by a commitment to collectivism, it is now necessary to ask what kind of collectivism the actives were in fact committed to.

Thus *CONCLUSION II* states that: *the belief that motivated the actives to participate was an intrinsic belief in trade unionism – a belief in the aims of trade-unionism as a social movement rather than an instrumental belief in trade unionism as a means of acquiring individual ends extrinsic to trade unionism – and was concerned with the trade union movement as a whole rather than the actives' own particular workplace affairs. For some actives, their intrinsic belief led directly to their participation; for others, a 'trigger' factor of some kind was needed to make their latent commitment manifest.*

and *CONCLUSION III* states that: *the actives' intrinsic belief in trade unionism embraced political and social goals as well as economic goals although the last were considered the most important.*

These two conclusions can be derived from the following survey findings:

(i)   that in a more detailed analysis of the reasons the actives gave for first joining a trade union, for first becoming active in a branch and for continuing to be active in their present branch, the majority of those actives giving 'collectivist' type answers referred to an intrinsic rather than to an instrumental belief in collectivism;

(ii)   that the majority of those actives classified as giving instrumental reasons for first becoming active referred, *not* to a belief in trade unionism of a limited and workplace orientated kind, but instead to a specific incident/ experience that led to them taking up participation on a permanent basis. This process was demonstrated by the increased proportion of actives giving intrinsic belief as the reason for their present level of branch activity. Actives who 'accidentally' became active appear to have gone through a closely similar process;

(iii)   that the inactives were of the opinion that the actives had an intrinsic belief or deep interest in trade unionism rather than an instrumental one.

(iv)   that the actives not only visualised the role of trade unions in British industrial life to be considerably greater than the inactives did, but they were more likely to consider that trade unions should play a role of some kind in British political and social life;

(v)   that the actives were much more likely than the inactives to feel that trade unions should try to change the present conditions of society in some way.

These survey conclusions are substantially supported by a number of scattered studies in the USA specifically on the characteristics of active and inactive trade union members, which have not been systematically related to each other before and which have been ignored by the proponents of the 'stake-in-the-job' and other previously reviewed theories. In particular we can note the work of Tannenbaum and Kahn (1958, pp.117–131, 148, 150), Rose (1952, pp.106–7) and Wilensky (1956, pp.117–8) in the USA, all of whom produced substantial empirical evidence showing that active members and shop stewards believed trade unions had, besides economic objectives, political and social goals such as working 'to improve the welfare of all people in the community', 'spending union funds to get laws friendly to labor' and working for equal wages for women in industry.[1] The survey findings are also supported in Great Britain by Goldstein's (1952, pp.261–8) work on the TGWU, where he empirically demonstrated that his small group of active members had a broader conception of trade union goals than the rank-and-file. They are further supported by Moran's (1974, pp.47, 111–2) rather more lightweight study of the UPW, where his 13 Manchester and Colchester branch officials were considerably more likely than the members of his Colchester rank-and-file sample both to have joined the UPW for 'moral' reasons of some kind, and to believe that the proper aims of the UPW included cultural as well as economic aims. Support is also provided by Beynon's (1973, pp.197–200) vividly painted but rather enumerate study of Ford workers in Liverpool, where it was the depth of commitment to trade unionism that distinguished his actives from the rank-and-file members, who tended to see their union merely in terms of a service organisation.[2]

More importantly, the survey conclusions are supported by Batstone et al.'s (1977, Chapter 2) careful study of shop stewards in vehicle manufacturing. These authors divided their shop floor stewards into types and while the 'populist' stewards (who lacked a commitment to trade unionism) were numerically the largest group, it was the second most numerous group, the 'leader' stewards, who took most part in branch affairs and were the most experienced and respected representatives. And it was this group which was most likely to believe workers should belong to a trade union to defend workers' rights and support socialism rather than to improve wages and conditions. The 'leader' stewards were also more likely to disagree that acting according to trade union principles was impractical and that union organisation above company level was irrelevant.[3] In the case of white-collar workers, we have Nicholson and Ursell (1977) who, in an article presenting some of the preliminary results from their study of NALGO members, suggest that their more active members view trade unions as having a wider role than solely defending job and pay levels. And finally, we have Reiner's (1978, pp.123–4) study of policemen in which he found an active core of 'Federationists' who were especially dedicated to the Federation and favoured it becoming like an ordinary trade union with full powers of industrial action.[4] Several of these authors (Moran, 1974, pp.127–8; Lipset et al. 1956, pp.406–7) specifically argued that a 'moral' or intrinsic commitment to trade unionism leads much more frequently to participation than does a concern solely with economic ends.

Having concluded that the actives felt that trade unions should pursue social and political as well as economic goals, the next conclusion defines the scope of such objectives. Thus *CONCLUSION IV* states that: *the goals the active steelworkers felt trade unions should pursue in the economic, political and social contexts, showed a concern with the improvement of the present social structure and not with the creation of a new social order.*

This conclusion can be derived from the following survey findings:

(i)   that in an analysis of the specific goals which the steelworkers felt trade unions should pursue in industrial, political and social life, the actives – along with those inactives who felt trade unions had a role of some importance in these areas – showed a preoccupation with the improvement of present wages and working conditions (often expressed as 'fairation'), with 'representation', with cooperation with the government in power/industry/ the public, and with the provision of a social milieu by trade unions for their members;

(ii)   that in a more detailed examination of the social changes the steelworkers felt trade unions should work for, the actives – along with those inactives who felt trade unions should work to some extent towards social change – felt trade unions should primarily concern themselves with the redistribution of wealth and income within present society, or with the improvement in the quality of today's working life.

There has been very little discussion, in any of the literature on trade unionism, about the scope of the ideological goals active members feel trade unions should pursue, so there is little here with which to compare the survey findings. However we can note that the views of the actives in the survey resembled those held by workers in Popitz et al.'s (1969, pp.288–93) study of the social imagery of West German steelworkers, specifically those workers with the 'second type' of dichotomous image (workers who saw society as an 'ordered structure' where the order was 'progressive' rather than 'static'). Workers with this second type of image included, as part of it, the view that the workers' share in present society was not sufficient and that the labour movement should provide the initiative in demanding a progressively increasing share for the working class. The link between Popitz et al.'s findings here and this survey is that these authors maintain that it was workers with the second type of image who, together with workers with their fifth type of image (those who saw society as a 'class society' in need of 'reform'), comprised the major part of those in their study committed to trade unionism.

Only the small-scale studies by Goldstein (1952, pp.261–8) and Moran (1974, pp.53, 112) provide any direct empirical evidence on the scope of actives' economic, political and social goals. And while Goldstein's work tends to support the survey findings – his active core had a conception of trade union goals which was wider than that of the rank-and-file but was by no means a radical one – Moran's work does not. The latter suggests that his branch officials felt trade unions as a social movement should work towards the achievement of radical cultural objectives such as a 'socialist world'.[5] Poole's comments on his engineering shop stewards in Sheffield are also interesting here and tend to agree with the general tenor of Goldstein's and of the present survey's findings. Poole (1974A, p.63) estimated that only a handful of his 'active negotiators and/or protectors of members' (his largest and most aggressive group of stewards) had a 'marked ethno-political philosophy', and saw themselves as part of a wider class in a 'Marxian sense'. Poole claimed that the majority of this type of steward (and of his other three types of steward), while aware of a measure of conflict implicit in their role, did not extend this to any wider critique of the socioeconomic system as a whole.

The actives' commitment to collectivism was shown in the present survey to be accompanied by a particular sociopolitical orientation that was not shared, or not shared to the same extent, by the inactives. Thus *CONCLUSION V* states that: *the actives tended to have a dichotomous image of society based on ideological criteria, while the inactives tended to have multi-class images based on material considerations. However, both groups were similar in, on the one hand, perceiving a clash of interests between the class groupings and, on the other (in apparent contradiction), perceiving a harmonious relationship between management and men in society. In greater contradiction still, the actives were a little more likely on balance to hold both of these perceptions than the inactives.*

75

This conclusion can be derived from the following survey findings:

(i)   that the actives' social images were significantly more likely to conform to Cousins' and Brown's Type A, while the inactives' images were fairly evenly divided between these writers' Types B to E, that the actives with Type A images most frequently referred to ownership of property and business as the main criterion for distinguishing between classes, while the inactives referred to money and standard of living;

(ii)   that half the inactives and just over half of the actives, in describing their social imagery, mentioned clashes of interest between the classes they envisaged as constituting present-day society, that most respondents in both groups, but particularly in the active, agreed that big business had too much power and disagreed that trade unions had too much, and that most in both groups, but particularly in the inactive, agreed that there was one law for the rich and one for the poor;

(iii)   that most of the respondents in both groups, but particularly in the active, felt that men and management could operate as a team, and that most respondents in both groups disagreed with the notion that management and men were on different sides.

There has also been very little specific research, in the literature on trade union participation, on active and inactive members' images of society with which to compare the results of the present survey, apart from some very generalised comments by writers in the USA suggesting that actives tend to view the working class as a significant reference group.[6] Popitz et al.'s (1969, pp.288–93) work on German steelworkers again, however, offers some parallels in the feelings of harmony between management and men among those workers with their second type of dichotomous image: these workers did not see the interests of employers and 'of the other side' to be in opposition to those of the working class, everyone with something to offer could obtain his share of it (it being understood that the share of the workers was still not large enough) and the authority of the employer was accepted as legitimate and non-exploitive. (But Popitz et al.'s findings do differ from those in the present survey, in that workers with their second type of image did not appear to perceive a more general clash of interest between classes in society, as those in this survey did. Thus, for example, the German steelworkers perceived financiers to have rights and functions as well as employers. Moreover, and perhaps more importantly, Popitz et al.'s non-participatory groups also held dichotomous images of society of some kind, not multi-class as the survey inactives tended to do.) Van de Vall (1970, p. 163) in his study of a Dutch trade union and a Dutch political party also provides some comparative material on the management/men relationship dimension: he clearly shows branch participants to have a more favourable opinion of 'present-day labor-management relations' than non-participants.[7]

However, Beynon's as well as Batstone et al.'s work suggests the opposite. Thus Beynon's (1973, p.197) shop stewards and actives had a more developed conflict image of the relationship between 'us', the workers, and 'them', the bosses, than did their rank-and-file members: they had an ideology of 'working class factory consciousness' where the employers together with the union bosses severely exploited the workers and the stage for this conflict was the factory floor. Similarly, Batstone *et al.* (1977, p.26) found that their 'leader-type' shop floor stewards, and in particular their 'quasi-elite' stewards (the most experienced and respected of all the 'leader-type' shop floor stewards) were much more likely than other types of steward to believe that workers have to fight bosses 'for everything'. In addition, Batstone *et al.* (p.125) at one point suggest that the 'quasi-elite' and 'leader' stewards had a more developed 'factory consciousness' – an awareness of the clash of interest between bosses and workers in the plant as a whole – than other types of stewards, whose collective interests were orientated towards their own section, a fact which sometimes endangered workers' unity at plant level by heightening sectional conflict.

CONCLUSION VI also deals with the actives' sociopolitical orientation and states that: *the actives were much more politically aware and interested than the inactives and more consistently supported the Labour Party. However, both groups had the same conception of the Labour Party as the representative of 'the working man' and the natural partner of the trade union movement.*

This conclusion follows from the survey findings:

(i)   that the actives were much more likely than the inactives to discuss politics;

(ii)   that the actives were much more likely than the inactives knowingly to pay the political levy;

(iii)   that the actives were more likely to vote consistently for the Labour Party in General Elections;

(iv)   that the majority of the actives and inactives in giving their reasons for voting for the Labour Party mentioned that it represented the interests of the working class;

(v)   that the majority of the actives and inactives believed that the trade unions should support the Labour Party.

There is a substantial amount of empirical evidence from studies of trade union participation supporting the survey findings here, showing that a commitment to intrinsic trade unionism has been associated with an awareness and understanding of the labour movement's role in politics and of current political issues. This is reflected, in Great Britain, by support of the Labour Party and, in the USA, by support of the Democratic Party. Thus, in the USA, Wilensky (1956, p.117) empirically shows committed actives to have a 'labor-liberal' political orientation, together with a high level of political awareness and interest. Kornhauser *et al.* (1956, pp.149–52) also empirically demonstrate that those with strong union attachment vote Democrat, have a strong 'pro-labor' orientation and a high degree of political interest. Lipset *et al.* (1956, p.101) clearly show that what they call 'high-liberal' ideologues were directly motivated by their values in their participation in the union. Finally, in the USA, Miller and Young (1955, pp.41, 45) describe (although without empirical substantiation) their 'small hard core' of meeting attenders as being very knowledgeable about trade unionism as a social movement.

In the UK, the government report *Workplace Industrial Relations* (1968, p.133) clearly shows shop stewards to be much more likely to pay the political levy. Cannon (1967, p.178) also clearly shows that, among printers, voting Labour is related to holding Chapel (union) office. Moran's (1974, pp.54, 112) study of the UPW showed his rather small group of branch officials to be considerably more in favour of trade union affiliation with the Labour Party than were his rank-and-file members; moreover, his branch officials saw this affiliation as central to their philosophy of unionism. It is also interesting to note that Lane and Roberts (1971, p.166) found, in their study of the 1970 unofficial strike at Pilkingtons, that of the 25 to 30 members of the rank-and-file strike committee all were Labour Party supporters, five were Labour members and two were Labour councillors. There are also a number of empirical studies that demonstrate the obverse of this relationship, i.e. that Labour Party actives are trade union members; while Denver and Bochel's study of blue-collar and white-collar Communist Party activists, Labour Party activists and Labour voters in Dundee, showed that political activism leads to trade union activism (Donnison and Plowman 1954, p.167; Bochel 1965, pp.38–9; Bealey *et al.* 1965 p.252; Denver and Bochel 1973, pp.66–7).[8]

On the other hand, the relationship between left-wing politics and trade union activism is disputed in the UK by Cousins (1972, p.226) in his study of shipbuilding workers on Tyneside. He claims that the shop stewards in his study were more likely to vote Conservative than were the rank-and-file, were less likely to pay the political levy and were more frequently able to state that they had definitely contracted out. However, a careful look at Cousins' data shows that only his claim on contracting out is actually viable in terms of statistical significance. This fact, coupled with Cousins himself finding no difference between shop stewards and workers in their belief that the connection between the trade unions and the Labour Party should be maintained, puts Cousins' general claim that shop stewards are less left-wing than their members in a dubious light. However, we should note that in two studies of British white-collar actives – Nicholson and Ursell (1977, p. 581) on local government officers and Reiner (1978, pp.125–6) on policemen – equal or greater numbers of trade union actives were said to support the Conservative Party. Although little substantial data was produced in either case, this does suggest that the link between white collar trade union activism and Labour Party support is less strong. However, and more in line with this survey's findings, Nicholson and Ursell suggest that their NALGO actives were more likely to have a general interest in politics and to belong to outside political organisations.

The survey findings indicated that the older and younger actives tended to derive their commitment to trade unionism from different sources. Thus *CONCLUSION VII* states that: *the older actives appeared to have derived their commitment to collectivism from their experiences of adversity, undergone as children in the context of a pro-union family, and from their own experience of striking and personal job grievances, undergone also in a pro-union context.*

This conclusion may be derived from the survey findings:

(i)   that the older actives were more likely than their inactive counterparts to have a father with major experience of being on strike;

(ii)   that the older actives were more likely than their inactive counterparts to have a father with major experience of being unemployed;

(iii)   that the older actives were very much more likely than their inactive counterparts to have been a child in a family that experienced 'hard times' due to the head of the household being on strike or unemployed;

(iv)   that the older actives were more likely than their inactive counterparts to have spent their childhood in a slum or near-slum;

(v)   that the older actives were significantly more likely than the inactives to have fathers and one or more siblings who strongly approved of trade unions and (if these were trade union members) who took an active part in branch affairs themselves;

(vi)   that the older actives were much more likely than their inactive counterparts to have some experience of being on strike themselves;

(vii)   that the older actives were much more likely than their inactive counterparts to have experienced a personal job grievance;

(viii)   that the older actives were more likely than their inactive counterparts to have one or more companions who strongly approved of trade unions and (if these were trade union members) who took an active part in branch activities themselves.

Finally, *CONCLUSION VIII* states that: *the younger actives, in common with the younger inactives, had no experiences of adversity. However, the younger actives appeared to be surrounded by pro-union persons: not only did they have pro-union fathers and siblings, but they also had pro-union work friends and leisure-time companions and it appears that they derived at least some of their commitment from association with these persons.*
This conclusion can be derived from the survey findings:

(i)   that the younger actives were more likely than their inactive counterparts to have pro-union and active kin;

(ii)   that the younger actives were also very much more likely than their inactive counterparts to have one or more work friends who strongly approved of trade unions and took an active part in branch affairs themselves;

(iii)   that the younger actives were very much more likely than their inactive counterparts to have one or more leisure-time companions who strongly approved of trade unions and (if trade union members) took an active part in branch affairs themselves.

We should note in connection with Conclusions VII and VIII that the older and younger actives, as well as deriving their commitment to collectivism in different ways, differed slightly in other contexts. The younger actives appeared a little more materialistic and instrumental and thus:

(i)   they differed more from their inactive counterparts than did the older actives and inactives in their view of how large a role trade unions should play in industrial life;

(ii)   they had compared with the older actives, a greater tendency, to give materialistic reasons for first joining a trade union;

79

(iii)   they appeared to have been much quicker-off-the-mark in getting a job at the steelworks – which offered excellent prospects in both cash and promotion terms – as soon as it opened, whereas the younger inactives tended to have arrived a year or two later and accordingly had lower seniority ratings.

However, the younger actives' slight tendency to instrumentalism is readily explainable by their marrying and starting their families earlier than their inactive counterparts.[9] Yet, despite these differences, older and younger actives had the same deep intrinsic commitment to trade unionism, the same view of which goals trade unions should pursue, and the same accompanying sociopolitical orientation. Nor did the older and younger actives differ in the extent to which their commitment either led them directly to activity or required a stimulus of some kind. Hence there is no reason to suppose that the next generation of trade union actives will differ significantly from the present in their 'core' attitudes towards trade unionism, even though the experiences of the 1920s and 1930s will be even more remote for them than they are for the present younger actives.

With regard to supporting evidence from the body of literature on trade union participation, some scattered pieces of empirical evidence can be collected to support the survey findings on the importance of experiences of adversity. Goldstein (1952, p.267) in the UK supplies the only substantive corroborating evidence here and he clearly demonstrated that his active members – interviewed in the late 1940s – were significantly more likely than his inactives to have been unemployed for more than six months continuously in the 1930s. Less specifically, Moran (1974, p.114) suggests that a radicalising experience in adolescence or early manhood can be 'translated' into trade union support; Batstone et al. (1977, p.26) suggest that harsh experience, or socialisation into a trade union tradition which emphasises such experience, is an important motivation for many shop floor stewards.[10] The only non-British material here is Chinoy's (1953, p.166) suggestion that experiences of unemployment and poverty in the 1930s in the USA may be a causal factor in participation. However, there is a good deal of empirical evidence in the UK produced in studies of political activism – those of Bochel (1965, pp.166, 170–3) on Ward Secretaries in the Labour Party in Manchester, Denver and Bochel (1973, pp.56–7) on Communists and Labour Party activists and members in Dundee, and Newton (1969, Chapter 3) in his study of the Communist Party – all showing experiences of hardship and unemployment (either at first hand as an adult or at second hand through a father's unemployment in the case of younger political party members) to be strongly associated with a commitment to political activism.[11]

With regard to the influence of members' families of origin there is some strong corroborating evidence from the USA in Seidman et al.'s (1958, p.174) work, which demonstrated a strong empirical relationship between having a father who was a trade union member and being a local leader in their miners', metal-workers' and plumbers' locals; their steelworker local was the only manual workers' local where there was no difference between the extent to which leaders and rank-and-file had fathers who were union members.[12] Moreover, Tannenbaum and Kahn's (1958, pp. 74–8) finding, of a significant relationship between being active and having a pro-union wife, supports the contention that the active's family of marriage can have a reinforcing effect on the active's commitment.

80

There is some rather tentative evidence in the UK supporting the present survey findings on the influence of active trade unionists' families. Thus Goldstein (1952, pp.265–7) gives some striking instances of union family upbringing leading to activity, and some data suggesting (but not statistically demonstrating) that his 'active core' were more likely than the rank-and-file to have fathers who were trade union members. Clegg (1954, pp.78–9) has some interesting comments to make on the existence of 'trade union families'. Beynon (1973, p.190) attaches importance to the fact that nearly 60 per cent of his stewards considered their fathers to be 'strong supporters of trade unionism'.[13] Moran (1974, p.112) found inheritance of trade union beliefs among his branch officials 'especially common', while Lane and Roberts (1971, p.166) found that about a third of their rank-and-file strike committee at Pilkingtons had relatives who had been active trade unionists.

The very tentative British findings reviewed above are considerably reinforced by Bochel's (1965, pp.54–7) findings on Labour Party activists, and by Denver and Bochel's (1973, pp.57–9, 63–4, 66) on Communist Party members, that family influence is very important in actives' first coming to support their party, as well as in the actives' actual joining of their party and in their continuing to be active in it. Both these studies make the point that, in addition to having family members who supported a political party and were considerably interested in politics, having a family member who was *active* in a political organisation was particularly important.[14]

With regard to the influence of work friends and leisure-time companions, Tannenbaum and Kahn's (1958, pp.82–5) work in the USA provides some corroborating evidence. These authors found a moderate relationship between union activity and having pro-union 'in-plant' and 'out-plant' friends. There is little in the UK literature on trade unionism here bar Moran's (1974, p.129) comment on the importance of the 'society of activists' (active postmen seeing each other outside of work and forming a cohesive social group) and Reiner's (1978, p.124) suggestion in his study of police unionism that trade union contact and experience in previous jobs can lead to activity in a new one. But Denver and Bochel's (1973, pp.60–66) work on political activism clearly shows 'peer groups', consisting of both workmates and friends, to play a part in political actives' first coming to support their party, in their actually joining the party and in their continuing to be active in it.

There is, however, an earlier finding in the survey that can now be incorporated into the discussion of the possible sources of the actives' commitment to collectivism. This is the finding, which applied equally to the older and the younger members in the survey, that activity was significantly related to skill. This was, it may be remembered, the most strongly supported survey finding when we considered the viability of the 'stake-in-the-job' theory. But this empirical relationship may be differently construed. There is a substantial suggestion, in both the British and the US literature, that not only does high skill status correlate with the possession of social and political skills, but also (and this is even more strongly supported) that low skill correlates with conformity, deference, and an acceptance of present conditions.[15] Hence it can be argued that the older actives were able, using their political and social skills, to build on to the predisposition towards trade unionism inculcated in them through their pro-union families of origin, by interpreting their experiences of adversity in line with the principles of trade-unionism and thus develop and reinforce an intrinsic commitment to it. Similarly, the younger actives were able, due to their political and social skills, to build quickly onto their familial predisposition, when they came into contact with trade union activities through their close network of pro-trade union companions and workmates and, in consequence, to develop the requisite commitment.

The contention that the actives possessed greater political and social skills – which enabled them to interpret their experiences or grasp principles – is significantly substantiated when we remember that the survey findings, as well as showing the actives to hold more skilled jobs than the inactives, also showed them to be both much more politically aware and interested and to participate much more readily in other formal associations. The latter finding may be remembered as the most strongly supported survey result when we considered the viability of the 'social activity' theory.

A second very important point regarding the actives' skill level also needs to be made here: that the greater political and social skills which the actives derived from their more highly-skilled jobs would have made it easier for them actually to participate in branch affairs, once they had built up their commitment to trade unionism and been consequently led to participate either soon after they had joined their first branch or after the occurrence of some incident that had made what had previously been their latent commitment manifest.

7

SOME WIDER IMPLICATIONS OF THE MODEL

There are now two questions that need to be asked of the model of participation presented in Chapter 6. We saw there that the 'intrinsic commitment to trade unionism' theory provides a satisfactory explanation for the participation pattern undertaken in the two Sheffield/Rotherham branches of BISAKTA that were the subject of this study. The first question to be raised is how likely is this model to prove applicable to other industrial situations? Points suggesting that the model might have wider application are: that the BSC Special Steels Division was at the time of the survey very much a going concern and not part of a declining traditional industry; and that the Sheffield/Rotherham conurbation, while being reasonably cosmopolitan, is not a newly developed area with a highly mobile population. On the other hand BISAKTA's conservative reputation may be a serious limiting factor in the model's wider application.[1] It could be argued that actives with moderate opinions predominated in the two BISAKTA branches in the study because their views fitted in with the overall ethos of their union: this could be because they had more or less consciously adopted this stance in order to be 'successful' as actives or because they had been moulded to be so by their union environment. This question could only be settled by a large-scale research project covering a number of industries and unions – preferably including some unions with a large proportion of white-collar or women members. Such a project would need to look in particular at causal factors in more detail than this study had the resources to pursue – especially in the case of the younger actives, the progenitors of future branch-level trade unionism. To develop a more complex causal model which could examine the interaction and diachronism of influences on and experiences of branch members, one would need not only to look at the most active and the most inactive members – as this study did – but also the middle ranges of activity; for instance, one should perhaps look for members with latent commitments to collectivism not yet precipitated into activity.

In such a large-scale survey, it is not impossible that several models of trade union activism with differing combinations of causal factors might be found. It is, for instance, likely that in certain industries, certain trade unions and certain geographical areas, the radical active would prove to be the norm. Again, in the case of skilled craft unions, skill level might be more important than collectivist commitment in distinguishing actives from inactives in a manner reminiscent of the 'stake-in-the-job' theory, the more highly skilled participating in order to protect their differential from attempts at erosion by their less skilled fellow union members: Turner's (1962, pp. 285–91) work on cotton unions would support this view.

The second question that needs to be asked of the model of branch participation presented here is: 'How does it relate to other more general models of grass-roots blue-collar trade unionism that have been described in the literature?' To begin with, it is clear that the survey findings on the kind of trade unionism adhered to by the Sheffield steelworkers, and its accompanying sociopolitical orientation, do not reflect the general picture of trade unionism in the traditional working class areas as described in such classical studies as those in Great Britain of Zweig (1952, pp. 177—9), Dennis *et al.* (1956, Chapter III) and Liverpool University's *The Dockworker*, and as summarised by Lockwood's (1966) widely-cited article.[2] These studies argue that certain industries tend to concentrate workers together in solitary communities, isolated from modern society in backwaters of industrial and urban development and that these communities develop the highest form of proletarian class consciousness, based on a sense of common identity and a shared picture of society as divided into two opposing classes, 'they' being persons in positions in which they can exercise power and authority over 'us'. The social order is seen as more or less immutable; wants and expectations are relatively fixed and life is orientated towards the present. These expectations, together with the stress laid on mutual aid and group solidarity, lead (the argument follows) to a trade unionism aimed at the protection rather than the development of collective interests and to an emphasis on collectivism as an end in itself (Lockwood 1966, pp.250—2; Goldthorpe *et al.* 1969, pp.118—9; Goldthorpe and Lockwood 1963, p.153; also Parkin 1971, pp.88—96). Such a view of trade unionism is accompanied, according to Goldthorpe *et al.*, by a longstanding support of the Labour Party as a political reflection of the 'us'/'them' class consciousness. Moreover, the alliance between the trade unions and the Labour Party is strongly approved, since they are seen as the industrial and political wings of an integrated labour movement (Goldthorpe *et al.* 1968B, p.75 and *The Dockworker*, p.132).

However, this view of trade unionism in traditional working-class areas has been disputed by Westergaard and Resler (1975, pp.394—5), who believe that the fatalistic and parochial character of trade unionism in these communities has been overemphasised. According to Westergaard and Resler, the British labour movement has always maintained its claim to work for a future socialist order, and has drawn on a class consciousness among ordinary manual workers which goes well beyond the parochial limits of locality, workplace and trade. Otherwise, they continue, the labour movement would never have been more than an alliance of 'village unions' linked for mutual defence, with neither wider objectives nor wider common loyalties to sustain them. In fact, the dichotomous class consciousness described by Bott and Hoggart – Lockwood's two main sources in his 1966 article – is too simplistic. Thus a look at Popitz *et al.*'s (1969) work in West Germany indicates that different sets of political beliefs are compatible with a dichotomous social imagery.[3] Popitz *et al.*, as well as finding one type of dichotomous consciousness among their steelworkers that closely resembled the fatalistic one described by Bott and Hoggart (Popitz *et al.*'s third type), also found present another type of dichotomous consciousness (their fifth type) that is compatible with Westergaard and Resler's arguments. The German steelworkers with this latter kind of image who were the 'last representatives of an ideological tradition whose sources lay in the past' saw trade unionism as a sociopolitical movement whose mission was the reform of the present unacceptable conditions of industry and society.[4] Thus Westergaard and Resler's argument that the consciousness of a significant body of traditional workers must differ from that of the classic descriptions of Bott and Hoggart appears to be a reasonable one. However, even if one modifies the description of traditional trade unionism to take account of Westergaard and Resler's criticism, the survey findings for the Sheffield steelworkers are still clearly divergent. The Sheffield steelworkers did not see the purpose of trade unionism to be that of fundamental social change: instead they wanted for trade union members and for the working class in general a better share of, and a better life in, the present social order.

As well as considering whether or not the trade unionism of the Sheffield steelworkers resembled that of the traditional proletarian worker, we need to compare their trade unionism with what is frequently described as 'business' or 'bread and butter' unionism; this type of unionism is said to be prevalent among blue-collar workers in the USA, and recently, instances of it have been described in Great Britain.[5] We can consider here how the Sheffield steelworkers compared to two specific 'tish studies of this type in the 1960s: that by Goldthorpe et al. (1968A) of xhall car workers, ball bearing workers and process workers in Luton, and that eynon (1973) of Ford car workers in Liverpool which was referred to earlier in chapter. Both of these studies showed blue-collar workers to have an economically workplace orientated trade unionism. Thus trade unions were considered to be economic bargainers concerned with pay, conditions of work and fringe benefits out not to be concerned with political or social change; trade unionism above the level of the workplace was thought irrelevant.[6] In addition to having an apparently similar trade union ideology, the Luton and Liverpool workers were also alike in terms of age, marital status and stage in family life cycle; furthermore, both groups had come to Luton or the Halewood Estate in Liverpool in search specifically of higher wages. These similarities make the widely differing sociopolitical orientations, within which their views on trade union roles were set, all the more surprising. These differing sociopolitical orientations suggest that there was a fundamental difference in the trade unionism of the Luton and Liverpool workers despite the superficial similarity.

Thus, the Luton workers' particularistic stance to trade unionism depended on a 'corporatist' approach to their firm: they had a 'teamwork' image of the relationship between management and workers and an appreciation of the extent to which their individual prosperity depended on the economic future of the firms they were presently employed in (Goldthorpe et al. 1969). The more general social imagery of the Luton workers was significantly different from that of the traditional proletarian and was closely related to their attitudes towards trade union functions and their employers. They saw society not as divided into two opposed classes but, instead, as consisting of a large central class which embraced the bulk of the salary and wage earners: only the very rich and the disadvantaged lay outside this class. The determinates of class position were not power or possession of the means of production but income, wealth, and standards of consumption. When it came to supporting and voting for a political party the Luton workers selected the Labour Party on the grounds that it was more likely to favour the material interests of the working class, or of themselves personally. However, this support was conditional on the Labour Party's performance and they perceived between the Labour Party and the trade unions 'no underlying ineluctable unity in their philosophies and goals'; indeed, they felt trade unions should keep out of politics.[7]

In sharp contrast, Beynon's activists and shop stewards, who strongly influenced and led the shop floor workers, had a view of management/worker relations as one of 'working class factory consciousness'. However, the shop stewards' and their members' class consciousness stopped short at the 'factory gate', and they had no clearly developed concept of politics. Instead of confidently picking the party that would materially benefit themselves most, the Liverpool workers were wary of political parties; they had abandoned their previous support of the Labour Party, which they judged had become revisionist, and now felt trade unions should leave party politics alone.[8]

The crux of the difference between the trade union ideology of the Luton and Liverpool workers is that Goldthorpe *et al.*'s Luton workers had an instrumental commitment to collectivism: they were concerned with the rewards collective action would confer on the individual and his nuclear family – collective action becoming the means for obtaining goals outside of the workplace. But it should be noted that even at its most instrumental, trade unionism was still important to the Luton workers and an integral part of their working lives.[9] In contrast, Beynon's Liverpool shop stewards had an intrinsic commitment to collectivism that clearly transcended the Luton workers' instrumentalism. Trade unionism represented, besides its economic and protection functions in the here and now, 'the struggles fought by workers over generations, it was a living tradition, based on collectivistic values of unity and brotherhood'. These stewards considered – although they felt it was of little relevance now – that the working class had been exploited by capitalists for centuries, and saw a need for revolution in an ultimate sense. The Liverpool shop stewards' commitment to trade unionism was thus bound up with their general ideology, and directed and enforced it. It should be noted that the Liverpool workers' commitment to trade unionism was intrinsic even though it concentrated on economic and protective functions only: in fact, trade unions were felt to be remarkably unsuited to changing the political and social conditions of society, since the trade unions' acceptance of capitalism made it difficult for them to resist their incorporation into the state. Social change for these stewards was the task of the Labour Party, but with this Party's renegation in the 1960s, the 'Halewood lads' were 'thrown back upon the trade unions and their grass roots organisations within them'.

However, the Sheffield steelworkers' trade unionism was not instrumental as the Luton workers' was, nor did they possess these workers' pecuniary imagery of a consensus society or their utilitarian approach to Labour Party support. The Sheffield workers' commitment to trade unionism was intrinsic as was that of the Liverpool workers, but the Sheffield workers' conception of trade union functions was considerably wider, including as it did social and political aims. Also in contrast to the Liverpool workers' retreat from politics and conception of trade unions as purely economic bargainers, and also to the Luton workers' feeling that trade unions should not be involved in politics, the Sheffield workers felt that the Labour Party and the trade unions could profitably work together to improve present conditions in society. Yet again the Sheffield workers' trade unionism was not wholly shop-orientated, as both the Luton and Liverpool workers' were: the Sheffield workers felt they had interests in common with workers in other plants and firms, and felt that trade unions should work to improve conditions for the whole working class in Great Britain. Finally, while the Sheffield steelworkers' image of society tended not to consist of a large central class but to be dichotomous as did that of the Liverpool workers, it was not nearly so disharmonious.

It is possible that the reason why the trade unionism of the Sheffield steelworkers does not correspond to either of the models of British and American blue-collar trade unionism reviewed above, is that writers such as Goldthorpe and his colleagues tend to conceive of solidaristic and instrumental trade unionism as a simple dichotomy: moreover, a dichotomy which is in the process of change from the predominance of radical and solidaristic trade unionism to the predominance of a limited instrumental trade unionism. Goldthorpe *et al.* (1969), in fact, believe that a significant change is taking place in the character of trade unionism and the meaning of trade union membership.[10] Thus Lockwood (1966, pp.254–8) in Britain sees once-widespread traditional proletarian attitudes on the wane, with the decline of industries such as mining and docking, with the absorption of working class enclaves into urban concentrations, and with the increase in residential mobility: working class affluence, the increase in the number of large factories with mass production techniques, and the development of private low-cost housing estates lead to the development of instrumentalism, privatism and pecuniary consciousness.

Mann and Giddens put forward more complex arguments, but both essentially maintain that radicalism in the labour movement is primarily a transitional phenomenon. Thus Mann (1973, Chapter 5) argues that the diversity of pre-industrial settings gave rise in the industrialising countries to a great diversity of ideological responses among workers and that some settings encouraged the emergence of revolutionary sentiments just as others encouraged the emergence of extremely conservative ones. But, according to Mann, as capitalism becomes hegemonic and eliminates 'archaic' institutions – as Mann feels it has done in Great Britain and the USA – the diversity of forms of organised consciousness declines, both radical and conservative, leaving the working class dominated by moderate, segmented and reformist ideology, which is typified for Mann by the consciousness of the Luton workers. Thus, within the trade union movement in Great Britain and the USA, radicalism – along with extreme conservatism – has declined, and a more limited and particularistic ideology now predominates. In France and Italy, however, Mann argues capitalism does not enjoy a hegemonic position – mainly due to employers' reluctance to act only within the narrowly capitalist frame of reference in relations with their employees – and in consequence the working class and the trade union movement in those countries have retained their radical (and extreme conservative) elements.

Giddens (1973, pp. 211–4, 257) argues that revolutionary class consciousness, should it occur, tends above all to characterise the *point of impact* of post-feudalism and capitalist-industrialism. It is not endemic to capitalist society, since it is class conflict which takes place in the context of 'contradictions' that is the primary determinant of revolutionary class consciousness. Once divergent class interests are recognised and formalised in collective bargaining, class conflict is controlled and outlets for it are provided, a process which undermines its revolutionary potential. The persistence of revolutionary consciousness in labour movements into modern times is a feature of societies (such as in France) which manifest 'uneven' development, since such societies have a long history of unresolved confrontation of 'progressive' capitalism and 'retroactive' semi-feudal agrarianism within a single overall national structure. However, Giddens argues that this radicalism is not simply the result of a lag in capitalist development which will soon be overcome, but that 'the mode of rupture with post feudal society creates an institutional complex, within which a series of profound economic changes are accommodated that then becomes a persisting system, highly resistant to major modification'.

Westergaard and Resler (1975, pp.389–92) challenge the assumption that popular radicalism is a transitional phenomenon which is being replaced, with the adoption of 'modern' production, by institutional class compromise. They point out that the labour movement in Great Britain has always had a *dual* orientation of radicalism and reformism. Thus they state that 'From the days of Chartism and before, labour's response to capital has been a mixture of defence and aggression; of pressures for recognition to protect wages, to keep work discipline at bay, with assertion of hopes for a society free of private capital; of routine co-operation, both with every-day subversion and principled denial of the legitimacy of business rule' (p. 390). Although these authors admit that 'defence has prevailed over attack in practice', they believe that capital is still as much under the 'threat of dispossession' today as it was in the times before the 1850s. Westergaard and Resler's duality argument for the British Labour movement – which they extend to all Western European highly industrialised countries – could, in addition, be applied to the labour movement in the USA. The radicalism of the early American trade unions and the 'Wobblies' has been well documented, and the work of writers such as Guérin suggests that radical elements still exist in American trade unions today.[11] These sources strongly contradict Hartz's argument that the USA's lack of a feudal tradition means that there has been no development of socialism or of a revolutionary trade union tradition.[12]

However, although Westergaard and Resler's argument that the consciousness of the labour movement in industrialised countries is not in a process of transition is a convincing one, it still implicitly accepts the radicalism/reformism dichotomy. The argument I put forward here is that a much wider variety of trade union ideologies is possible, certainly in Great Britain. The moderate 'social improvement' orientated trade union ideology of the Sheffield steelworkers and Beynon's car workers' economic ideology are examples. Indeed one can argue further that the trade union ideology of the Sheffield steelworkers might, in a large scale survey, prove to be one of the dominant types of trade union ideology in British industries not characterised by isolated, solidary communities or by recent rapid development. It is also possible that such a moderate 'social improvement' ideology may have been widely adhered to in the past in the British trade union movement. We can therefore adopt Westergaard and Resler's valid historical argument and maintain that a 'social improvement' ideology does not represent the breakdown of an earlier more radical type of trade union ideology; and it also follows that this ideology is not itself in the process of breaking down into a more economic and particularistic one. Indeed the work of researchers such as Brown and his colleagues (Cousins and Brown 1972; Brown *et al.* 1972; Brown and Brannen 1970) on shipbuilding workers on Tyneside, and Moore's (1975) on miners in Durham, strongly suggests that proletarian traditionalism may not be as typical of such industries as is thought, while recent studies of unemployment, such as that by Marsden and Duff, indicate that work is still today an important experience and source of social rewards for many workers.[13] It can even be argued that the instrumental consciousness of the Luton workers was not a signpost to the future but the product of a very specific period of affluence, full employment and consensus politics during the early 1960s.[14]

We must also, in our consideration of the relationship between the findings of the survey of Sheffield steelworkers and other general models of grass-roots blue-collar trade unionism consider the idea, put forward most coherently and controversially by Mallet (1975) in France, that present-day trade unionism is developing in a new direction due to the introduction of automated technology. This idea explicitly counters the arguments of the largely American theorists in the 1950s and early 1960s, such as Blauner, who claimed that with automation trade unions lose the greater part of their functions and begin to decline due to the main sources of grievance generated by the work task being eliminated, to workers gaining both high wages and a high level of job security, and to workers of all levels increasingly identifying with their firm and management.[15] The 'trade unions in decline' theory will not be examined here since, with the exception of Blauner (whose methodology is far from satisfactory) these US writers were not concerned with the investigation of the attitudes of trade union members on the shop floor.[16]

Mallet contrasts his idea of a new development in trade unionism with what he sees as French trade unionism in the first half of the twentieth century: mass union organisation controlled by highly centralised bureaucracies and characterised by fragmentary, short-lived and mostly unsuccessful strikes, primarily directed to increasingly restricted economic ends. Mallet believes that the development of automation transforms social relations at work, leads to profound changes in the attitudes and aspirations of the workforce and hence has major implications for the character of the trade union movement. Mallet describes the new radical form of trade unionism that develops as the result of workers becoming aware of their alienation, as 'company level trade unionism' which, while it rediscovers on the organisation level some of the features of craft unionism, is not the 'rebirth of syndicalism with a modern face'. Indeed the main features of this company-level trade unionism are: (1) the regeneration of trade unionism with workers in the advanced sector being far more likely to become unionised and active; (2) the tendency for trade union activities to be based on the company, that is the company as an economic unit, and not on the particular plants/factories comprising it; and (3) the formulation of demands by the trade union movement for control over technical conditions of production and over economic aspects, such as the nature of investment and market orientation.[17] Mallet notes developments in France which he believes mark stages in the emergence of these new lines of trade union action, particularly the demand for control over company management. Thus he notes: (1) the development of the idea that company agreements are bound to be substituted for the former branch and local agreements; (2) the development of a new concept of strike action – 'scientific striking'; (3) the development of trade union unity on the shop floor; (4) the adoption of a single trade union structure; and (5) the feeling by the militant workers of an absolute need to know the market mechanisms and financial management of the company, which implies a revaluation of the role of the plant committee and leads to trade unions debating the company's management policy.

Mallet produces very little evidence himself to substantiate his argument on the development of trade unionism with the introduction of automation. However, two authors who set out to test empirically the 'new working class' theory provide relevant material here for examination: these were Durand and Gallie. Durand (1971A) undertook two studies, the first of which, on the nature of strikes in May 1968 in the traditional and technical sectors of French industry, was rather lightweight.[18] But Durand's (1971B) second study possessed a more complex methodology involving interviewing over 1,000 trade union 'militants'. The focus of Durand's research here was to see if trade union militants in the technical sector of French industry could be more frequently classified as having a 'C3 model' of trade unionism – a unionism of planning and control – than could workers in the craft or mass production sectors. Durand in fact showed that 35 per cent of his technical workers had a view of trade unionism corresponding to his 'C3 model', compared to 20 per cent of his craft workers and 19 per cent of his mass-production workers. However, Gallie (1978, pp.320–2) in his excellent critique of Durand's second study, points out: (1) the inadequacy of Durand's questions in the light of the complexity of his theoretically-derived models – consisting as they did of the actor's self-image, his image of his opponent and his overall conception of society; (2) the general lack of internal consistency between Durand's indicators (militants' attitudes on 15 substantive issues) for his models; (3) the fact that Durand's retention of only those indicators with good interrelationships for each particular model led to militants being classified on the basis of answers to non-comparable issues; (4) the gap between Durand's retained indicators for each model and his original theoretical conception of it; (5) the ambiguity of Durand's crucial 'category C3', which grouped militants in the Moderate Confederation Generale des Cadres (whose prime interest was in economic planning) together with militants in the Confederation Française Democratique du Travail (who were interested in both 'democratic planning' and enterprise control); and (6) Durand's loose definition of the technical sector compared to Touraine's original conception in 'La Conscience Ouvrière'. Gallie concludes that Durand's measuring instruments are likely to be distorted; and since the differences Durand found between the trade union models held by militants in the craft, mass-production and technical sectors were fairly small, Gallie believes that the risk for the overall conclusion of any distortion is maximised, and hence that 'it would be wisest to assume that the implications of advanced technology for the pattern of unionism remains an open question'.

Gallie's own work produces fewer methodological problems. The part of his research that concerns us here is his question as to whether the growth of a highly automated sector of industry has major implications for the nature of trade unionism, or whether trade unionism in that sector is assimilated into the wider patterns of the society.[19] Gallie believes that to decide between these two propositions, a cross-cultural study of two countries characterised by advanced capitalism was necessary – where cultural factors, particularly the pattern of class relations, would be varied while technological ones could be kept constant: hence Gallie's choice of oil-refinery workers in France and Great Britain.

Gallie convincingly shows in his work, contrary to both Blauner's and Mallet's predictions, that automation has had little significant impact on the pattern of trade unionism in Britain or France. Rather, the author shows that in the wider society powerful trade unions, with their long established traditions and well-set modes of ideology and organisation, have succeeded in penetrating the advanced sector and have assimilated it into broader social patterns.[20] Hence it follows, as Gallie found, that France and Great Britain had fundamentally different patterns of trade unionism, neither of which significantly resembled Mallet's conception of a new radical 'company-level' trade unionism.[21] Thus in the French refineries, Gallie found the actives to be heavily influenced by the unions' central apparatus and to see their primary task as one of heightening the consciousness of the workforce, so that its members could understand the extent of their alienation within capitalist society and seek a major transformation of the basic institutional structure of society. The local actives' strategy for achieving this was one of sustained ideological warfare in the context of steadily escalating action over concrete disputes with management; the actives advanced specific demands that linked, in a complex way, societal and local issues and involved a systematic attempt to bring the workforce into periodic confrontation with the government. In contrast, in the British refineries, the actives were mainly influenced by shop floor opinion and saw their task as one of representing the workforce, of forwarding objectives that were consciously and explicitly desired by the workers themselves. These objectives were in no way concerned with significant structural change in society but, instead, were simply formulated and narrow in scope. The local actives' strategy for achieving this task was the building up of a powerful, well-disciplined and cohesive organisation, which would represent such a potential threat in the event of conflict that management was unlikely to risk being recalcitrant in negotiations. To achieve this, the local actives were prepared to see the development of a system of exchange with management: management helping the trade union officials in building up organisation strength and trade unions helping management in control of the workforce. Thus, overall, in French trade union terms the British actives were allowing and even contributing towards the progressive integration of workers within the existing structure of capitalist society.

Hence according to Gallie, the nature of trade unionism in France and Britain is fundamentally different, always has been so, and will continue to be so in the future since the social structure and cultural pattern of the two countries differ so markedly.[22] The interesting question to ask now, and which Gallie does not tackle, is how much variation in the nature of trade unionism is possible within one country, and whether the radical/reformist character of trade unionism proposed by Westergaard and Resler, or the moderate 'improvement-orientated' trade union consciousness put forward by the present study, can be incorporated within Gallie's national picture. Superficially, Gallie's British refinery workers – all members of the TGWU – resemble Goldthorpe *et al.*'s affluent workers in Luton in their economic and shop-orientated trade union consciousness. But a closer reading of Gallie's work reveals definite hints that the British refinery workers held a view of trade unionism significantly wider than that of the Luton workers. There are indications in Gallie's work that participation in the TGWU branches in the refineries would involve contact with the ideas: that a trade union should strive to control the industry in which its members were engaged; that shop stewards should strive for control over everyday management powers; that a trade union should try to improve its members' lot by linking itself to the Labour Party; and that a trade union should be concerned with social intercourse among members.[23] Thus it can be argued that the trade unionism of Gallie's oil refinery workers more closely resembles the 'improvement-consciousness' model than it did the reformist or radical one, thereby suggesting that the model developed from this study of Sheffield steelworkers can apply more widely to other union and industrial situations.

The answer to the second question asked in this chapter, 'How do the findings on the survey of Sheffield steelworkers relate to other more general models of trade unionism that have been presented in the literature?' can now be briefly stated. The moderate 'improvement-conscious' model of trade unionism developed from the survey findings differs in significant respects from traditional unionism, 'business unionism' and Mallet's radical unionism. Thus, the steelworkers' belief in trade unionism was intrinsic, a belief in the aims of trade unionism as a social movement rather than, as in the case of the 'business unionist', an instrumental belief in trade unionism as a collective means of acquiring extrinsic, individual ends. This belief was also concerned with attaining the ends of the trade union movement as a whole rather than those of an active's company (as in Mallet's radical unionism) or his own particular workplace (as in 'business unionism'). Secondly, the steelworkers' intrinsic belief in trade unionism embraced political and social goals, as well as economic ones. While traditional unionism and Mallet's radical unionism also encompassed political and social goals, the emphasis in these two models on such goals is greater than it is in the steelworker's model of unionism: for the steelworkers economic goals were clearly given precedence. Finally, the nature of the political and social goals of trade unionism also differed between the steelworkers' model of unionism and that of the traditional and automated industry workers: the steelworkers were concerned with the improvement of the present social structure and not with the creation of a new social order. I argue there is a strong likelihood that the predominant type of blue-collar trade union ideology in British industry (both today and in the past) significantly resembles the Sheffield steelworkers' moderate, 'improvement-conscious' unionism, while other suggested forms are the products of specific and atypical work and community milieux or are unlikely to come about in the foreseeable future.

APPENDIX 1
THE PARTICIPATION QUESTIONNAIRE SURVEY

Each member of the two branches selected for the study received a copy of the questionnaire accompanied by an introductory letter on a separate sheet. The letter was personally addressed to each branch member, whereas the questionnaire bore only the member's code number. This letter explained that the survey was being made by an independent research worker and that both the BISAKTA officials and BSC's management had given their approval. In asking for the member's cooperation, the confidentiality of the questionnaire was emphasised.

The questionnaires were placed in large brown unsealed envelopes, together with copies of the introductory letter. The members' names were written on gummed labels which were attached by one corner to the envelopes. These envelopes were then handed out by the branch officials on each shift and in each department to the individual members. In addition the branch officials agreed to 'put in a good word' informally for the survey. The respondents, as requested in the introductory letter, replaced the completed questionnaires (but not the introductory letters) in the en-velopes, sealed them and tore off the gummed labels. They then handed the envelopes either to the branch official who originally gave them to them or to their branch secretary.

The participation survey of the Bloom and Billet Mill was carried out during December 1970 and January 1971, and that of the Melting Shop during June and July 1971. The response rates were very satisfactory in both workshops, particularly so for a self-completed questionnaire. Of the 126 members currently working in the Melting Shop, 118 responded and 8 did not, giving a response rate of 94 per cent. Of the 166 members currently working in the Bloom and Billet Mill, 151 responded and 15 did not, giving a response rate of 91 per cent. The response rate for the two branches combined was 92 per cent.[1]

It was possible to compare the respondents and non-respondents with respect to their departments, shifts, dates of birth, skill level and length of time they had been employed at the steelworks. In the case of the non-respondents, this information was available from the firm's records. In fact, no significant difference was found between the respondents and non-respondents with respect to any of these social characteristics. The two branch secretaries were also asked to give their opinion on how much the non-respondents in their respective branches took part in branch affairs; they were given 6 answers to choose from, including a 'don't know' category. Here it was found, not surprisingly, that none of the non-respondents was rated as doing a 'great deal' for the branch. Three of the non-respondents were rated as doing a 'fair amount' and four as doing 'a little'. Most of the non-respondents, however, were rated as doing 'nothing much' or 'nothing at all'.[2]

The introductory letter and participation questionnaire are reproduced below. However, for reasons of space, the various grids on which the respondent recorded his replies on the participation questionnaire have been omitted. There were some variations between the participation questionnaires for the two branches in detail such as number of shop meetings held recently. Where there is such a difference, the Melting Shop alternative is given first. Table A1.1 summarises the findings of the participation survey for the various questions.

Introductory Letter for Participation Survey

University of Cambridge
Faculty of Economics and Politics

Telephone (0223) 58944

Sidgwick Avenue,
CAMBRIDGE,
CB3 9DD

14 June 1971
12 November 1970

Dear Mr.

I am an independent research worker from Cambridge University and I am conducting a survey of your branch. Mr. White, the district secretary, Mr. Smith, your branch secretary, Mr. Jones, the manager of the shop/mill, and Mr. Brown the personnel manager, have all agreed to my survey and are helping me. I hope you can help me by answering as carefully and as fully as you can the enclosed questions about your branch activities. It is very important for the research that everybody in the branch completes the questionnaire and I am most anxious for your cooperation. I am interested in those who do not participate as well as those who do.

All the answers you give will be strictly confidential. Only I know your particular code number. No one in the union or B.S.C. will ever know how you personally answered the questions.

When you have filled in the questionnaire, please replace it in the envelope, seal the envelope and remove the name label. Do not enclose this letter. Then return the envelope and contents as soon as you can either to the branch official who gave it to you, or to Mr. Smith.

Thank you very much.

Yours faithfully,

Patricia Fosh, B.A.(Econ.), Sheffield.

The Participation Questionnaire

Please can you answer the following questions.

Where a choice of answers is given, please answer by ticking in the appropriate box or boxes.

1. Department:
2. Shift A, B, C or D

3. Date of birth
4. Place of birth (country and city/town/nearest town)
5. Job in the (Melting Shop)
   (Bloom and Billet Mill)
6. How long have you worked at the steelworks?
7. How often do you go to branch meetings? Regularly, fairly regularly, sometimes, rarely, never?
8. Did you go to the last branch meeting on (May 22nd 1971)?
   (October 11th 1970)?
9. If you go to branch meetings 'sometimes' or more frequently, how much would you say you talked at them? Talk a great deal, talk a fair amount, say something occasionally, rarely say anything, never say anything?
10. Do you go to shop meetings when they are held? Always go, usually go, sometimes go, rarely go, never go?
11. Did you go to the shop meeting held in March to discuss the redundancy issue?
    Or
    How many of the four shop meetings held in August to discuss the new tonnage bonus did you go to?
12. If you go to shop meetings when they are held 'sometimes' or more frequently, how much would you say you talked at them? Talk a great deal, talk a fair amount, say something occasionally, rarely say anything, never say anything?
13. How often do you vote in elections for union officers? Regularly, fairly regularly, sometimes, rarely, never?
14. Did you vote in the last election for union officers in (December 1970)?
    (November 1969)?
15. Did you ask the branch to take up any grievance on your behalf during this last year ending in (May)?
    (November)?
    (This refers to *personal* grievances that you yourself took up if you are a branch official).
16. If you answered 'yes' to Question 15, how many grievances did you ask the union to take up (or how many *personal* grievances did you take up yourself if you are a branch official)?
17. Have you attended any educational courses on trade unionism?
18. If you answered 'yes' to Question 17, please could you tick the appropriate course or courses listed below.
    University of Sheffield Extramural Studies 'Trade Unions and Industrial Relations in the Steel Industry'.
    Worker's Educational Association 'Industrial Relations for Trade Unionists'.
    Richmond College 'Industrial Relations'.
    Industrial Society 3 day 'Trade Union course'.
    Granville College of Further Education 'Short Courses for Trade Unionists'.
    Trades Union Congress Education Service
    1. *Linked Weekend Courses*
       'Shop Stewards and Workplace Representatives Training'

'Work Study for Trade Unions'
'Trade Unions and the Economy'
'Productivity Bargaining – Job Evaluation and Merit Rating'
'Industrial Democracy'
'Management Techniques for Trade Unions'
'Prices, Incomes and Productivity Bargaining'
2. *Single Weekend Schools*
'Branch Chairmanship'
'Trade Union Representation on Local Tribunals'
'Industrial Relations and the Law'
'Company Accounts and Costing for Trade Unionists'
'Branch Committee Meetings and Conference Procedure'
Other – please specify.

19.   Are you on any BISAKTA committees *this year*?

20.   If you answered 'yes' to Question 19, please could you tick the appropriate committee or committees listed below.
(Melting Shop Branch Committee)
(Bloom and Billet Mill Branch Committee)
Steelworks Joint Committee
Sheffield Joint Committee
Sheffield Negotiating Committee
(Melting Shop Consultative Committee)
(Bloom and Billet Mill Consultative Committee)
Steelworks Section Council
Working Party for Joint Consultation
Other – please specify

21.   Have you ever been on any other union committees *before this year*?

22.   If you answered 'yes' to Question 21 please could you tick the appropriate committee or committees listed below
(Melting Shop Branch Committee)
(Bloom and Billet Mill Branch Committee)
Steelworks Joint Committee
Sheffield Joint Committee
Sheffield Negotiating Committee
(Melting Shop Consultative Committee)
(Bloom and Billet Mill Consultative Committee)
Steelworks Section Council
Working Party for Joint Consultation
Other – please specify

23.   Do you hold any official BISAKTA position *this year*?

24.   If you answered 'yes' to Question 23, please could you tick the appropriate position or positions listed below.
Branch Chairman
Branch Vice-Chairman
Branch Secretary
Branch Shop Representative
Steelworks Joint Committee Chairman

96

Steelworks Joint Committee Vice-Chairman
Steelworks Joint Committee Secretary
Sheffield Joint Committee Chairman
Sheffield Joint Committee Vice-Chairman
Sheffield Joint Committee Secretary
Other — please specify.

25. Have you ever held any official positions in any union *before this year*?
26. If you answered 'yes' to Question 25, please could you tick the appropriate position or positions listed below.
BISAKTA Branch Chairman
BISAKTA Branch Vice-Chairman
BISAKTA Branch Secretary
BISAKTA Branch Shop Representative
Steelworks Joint Committee Chairman
Steelworks Joint Committee Vice-Chairman
Steelworks Joint Committee Secretary
Sheffield Joint Committee Chairman
Sheffield Joint Committee Vice-Chairman
Sheffield Joint Committee Secretary
Other — please specify
27. How familiar are you with the contents of BISAKTA's Rule Book? Very well acquainted with the contents, know the contents fairly well, know roughly what the contents are, know a little about the contents, don't know anything about the contents, didn't know there was a Rule Book?
28. How often do you read *Man and Metal*? Regularly, fairly regularly, sometimes, rarely, never, never heard of *Man and Metal*?
29. If you read *Man and Metal* 'sometimes' or more frequently, how much of it do you read? All, most of it, certain parts, (please specify which), little bits of it (please specify which), only really glance at the cover?
30. How often do you talk to your workmates about union affairs either at work or when you are away from work? A great deal, a fair amount, now and then, rarely, never?
31. And when did you last talk to your workmates about union affairs?
32. How often do you talk to your branch officials or committeemen about your work and conditions? A great deal, a fair amount, now and then, rarely, never?
33. And when did you last talk to any branch officials or committeemen about your work and conditions?
34. How much do you help canvass in the elections for Executive Council members? Always, usually, sometimes, rarely, never, didn't know there were any elections for Executive Council members?
35. If you do help canvass, did you do so in the last election held in January 1970?

Thank you for helping me.

The scoring method
In the scoring of the participation questionnaire, the formal and informal

Table A1.1 *Summary of level and pattern of participation in the Melting Shop and Bloom and Billet Mill*

Question number	Selected measure	Melting Shop			Bloom and Billet Mill		
		%	N		%	N	
7	'Regularly' or 'fairly regularly' attends branch meetings	66	56	117	29	19	50
8	Attended last branch meeting	36	31	117	18	12	150
9	Talks a 'great deal' or a 'fair amount' at branch meetings	26	23	113	18	18	98
10	'Always' or 'usually' attends shop meeting when held	68	58	117	78	52	149
11	Attended recent shop meeting (Melting Shop) or attended one or more of four recent shop meetings (Bloom and Billet Mill)	88	75	117	77	52	149
12	Talks a 'great deal' or a 'fair amount' at shop meetings	30	28	107	19	17	111
13	'Regularly' or 'fairly regularly' votes in elections for union officers	64	55	116	41	28	149
14	Voted at last election for union officers	62	53	116	36	24	148
16	Asked the branch to take up one or more grievances during the past year	24	20	117	32	21	150
18	Attended one or more educational courses on trade unionism	5	4	117	9	6	151
20	Are on one or more BISAKTA committees present year	12	10	117	10	7	151
22	Have been on one or more BISAKTA committees before present year	23	20	117	31	20	151
24	Hold one or more BISAKTA positions present year	5	4	116	6	4	151
26	Held one or more BISAKTA positions before present year	13	11	117	28	19	151
27	'Very well' or 'fairly well' acquainted with the contents of BISAKTA's rule book	30	26	117	35	23	151
28	'Regularly' or 'fairly regularly' read *Man and Metal*	36	31	117	18	12	151
29	Read 'all' or 'most' of *Man and Metal*	52	52	100	31	67	46
30	Talk to workmates about union affairs a 'great deal' or a 'fair amount'	44	38	117	61	40	151
31	Talked to workmates about union affairs within last three days	36	32	111	45	33	137
32	Talk to branch officials or committeemen about work and conditions a 'great deal' or a 'fair amount'	38	32	117	31	20	151

Table A1.1*(cont.)*

Question number	Selected measure	Melting Shop			Bloom and Billet Mill		
33	Talked to branch officials or committee men about work and conditions within last three days	47	46	103	42	34	125
34	'Always' or 'usually' help canvass in the elections for Executive Council members	6	5	117	6	4	149
35	Helped canvass in last election for Executive Council members	4	3	117	8	6	149

aspects were given, as far as possible, equal weighting. An attempt was also made here to balance up the 'costs' of the different forms of participation and to take some account of past activities as well as present. For the formal aspects, questions 7, 9, 13 16,18,20,22,24 and 26 were used. For the informal aspects, questions 10,12,27,28, 30,32 and 34 were used.

For questions 7,9,10,12,27,28,30,32 and 34 the first two answers scored 2, the third answer scored 1 and the last two answers scored 0.

For question 16, 1 was scored for each personal grievance the respondent asked the branch to take up during the previous year. This question created difficulties in the case of five respondents who said that they had placed a very much higher number of personal grievances than was anticipated in devising the scoring system; one respondent, in fact, said he had placed over 50 personal grievances. Not surprisingly, these five respondents accumulated high enough scores to be classified as active. However, when their scores for question 16 were subtracted, all but one of the five still scored enough to be classified as active. This one exception was excluded from the active group, as his replies to the other questions were more typical of the middle range scorers than of the other actives.

For question 18, 1 was scored for each education course attended. No difficulties arose here.

For questions 20,22,24 and 26, 2 was scored for each committee the respondent was on and for each position he held, with the exception, however, of those answers which were concerned with joint consultation committees and consequently did not receive any score. Any answers filled in in the 'other' categories in question 20 and 24, which did not refer to BISAKTA committees or positions, did not receive a score. Similarly, any answers filled in in the 'other' categories in questions 22 and 26, which did not refer to union committees or positions in a union previously belonged to by the respondent, did not receive a score.

APPENDIX 2
THE INTERVIEW SURVEY

The active and inactive members of the two branches, as selected by the participation questionnaire survey analysis, were all sent an introductory letter asking for their agreement to be interviewed. This letter reassured the potential respondents: (1) that the survey was being conducted with the support of both management and union officials; and (2) that all the interviews would be conducted with strictest confidence. The respondents were interviewed in the case of the Bloom and Billet Mill from August to November 1971 and in the case of the Melting Shop from January to April 1972, during working hours in spare offices in the Melting Shop and Bloom and Billet Mill office blocks which were sited next to their respective shops. Each interview lasted from an hour to an hour and a half. The response rates for both active and inactive respondents were very high: 66 out of 67 (98.5 per cent) active respondents agreed to be interviewed as did 59 out of 63 (94 per cent) inactive ones.[1]

The interview schedule utilised a number of different measuring techniques including scaling measures, agreement/disagreement statement-type questions, pre-coded limited choice questions and open-ended questions. Some of the open-ended questions were used as lead-ins to relatively unstructured discussions of the more sensitive and exploratory areas of the interview, which were tape-recorded.

The interview schedule and introductory letter are reproduced below. However, the various charts and grids, on which the respondent's replies to a number of the questions were recorded, are omitted for reasons of space.

The notes in brackets are instructions to the interviewer. These indicated when the question required the handing of a prompt card to the respondent, and when the respondent's reply was to be tape-recorded. The prompt cards used in the survey in all cases duplicated the wording printed on the schedule.

Introductory letter for interview survey
University of Cambridge
Faculty of Economics and Politics

Sidgwick Avenue,
CAMBRIDGE,
CB3 9DD.

Telephone (0223) 58944

Dear Mr.

I am an independent research worker from Cambridge University and I am conducting a survey of your branch. Mr. White, the district secretary, Mr. Smith, the branch secretary, Mr. Jones, the Melting Shop/Bloom and Billet Mill manager, and

Mr. Brown, the personnel manager, have all agreed to my survey and are helping me. You helped me very greatly in June/December by filling in for me a questionnaire on your branch activities. I have selected 50 names at random from the branch to interview. Your name was one of those which was chosen by chance.

I hope that you can help me again by agreeing to my interviewing you. Mr. Jones has given me permission to interview you during working hours and I can arrange a time to suit your convenience. I am most anxious for your cooperation because no other name can be substituted for yours. Everything you say at the interview will be completely confidential. No-one in the union or B.S.C. will ever know how you personally answer the questions I ask you.

I shall contact you in the near future to make arrangements for the interview.

Thank you very much,

Yours sincerely,

Patricia Fosh, B.A. (Econ.), Sheffield.

Interview schedule

First of all I would like to ask you some questions about your *present job*.

Listed below on this interview schedule are a number of questions about your job. Below each question, there is a scale which ranges from 'First rate' to 'Very poor'. For each question please can you indicate how you personally rate this aspect of your job by placing an X at the appropriate point on the scale. (Show scales to respondent.)

1. How do you rate the *interest* and *variety* in your present job?

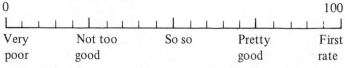

Very poor	Not too good	So so	Pretty good	First rate

2. How do you rate the *opportunity to use skill* in your present job?[2]
3. How do you rate the opportunity *to use your own initiative and take responsibility* in your present job?
4. How do you rate your *wages* in your present job?
5. How do you rate the *security* of your present job?
6. How do you rate the *friendliness, sociableness and pleasantness* of your workmates?
7. How do you rate the *job that your BISAKTA branch is doing* in looking after the branch members' interests?
8. (1) How do you rate your *relationship with your shift foreman*?
    (2) Why do you think you get on with your foreman in this way?

Still talking about your *present job*, I am going to ask you some questions that have 5 possible answers. I will hand you a card with the answers written on; please can you tell me which answer corresponds most closely to your own feelings.

9. How often do you talk to your workmates in general? A very great deal, quite a lot, to some extent, not very much or not at all? (Hand prompt card.)
10. Some jobs *allow* people to talk to each other more than others depending on how near you work to other people, how noisy the place is, how much

you have to concentrate and how much walking about you do, how much talking to other people *can* you do while you are working? A very great deal, quite a lot, to some extent, not very much or not at all? (Hand prompt card.)

11. How would you feel if you were moved to another job still at (steelworks) similar to the one you're doing now and with the same pay, but away from the people you now work with? Very upset indeed, pretty upset, a little upset, not very much upset or not upset at all? (Hand prompt card.)

12. How much interest do you feel that the management at (steelworks) take in you as a person? A great deal of interest, quite a bit of interest, a certain amount of interest, not very much interest or no interest at all? (Hand prompt card.)

13. (1) How would you say B.S.C.'s management compares to the managements at other firms in this area? Very much better, quite a bit better, about average, quite a lot worse or very much worse? (Hand prompt card.)
    (2) Why did you give that answer?

14. How often do you talk about work outside of work to your family and friends? A great deal, quite a lot, to some extent, not very much or not at all? (Hand prompt card.)

15. (1) Are there any people you work with whom you consider to be *close friends*, rather than just workmates or members of management staff?
    (2) (If yes, ask:)
        (1) Please could you give me their names, so that we can sort them out in these boxes? (Explain to respondent that names are required so that their participation scores can be looked up later. Emphasise confidentiality.)
        (2) Is X a shop-floor worker or a member of management?
        (3) Do you see X outside of work regularly?
        (4) Does X live in your neighbourhood? (i.e. within about 10 minutes' walking distance.)
        (5) How do you think X feels about trade unions in general? Strongly approves, mildly approves, is neither for nor against, mildly disapproves, strongly disapproves or don't you know? (Hand prompt card.)
        (6) (If management friend belongs to a trade union branch or if workmate friend belongs to a trade union branch that is not respondent's own branch, ask) How much would you say X does for this branch? A great deal, a fair amount, a little, not very much, nothing at all or don't you know? (Hand prompt card.) Does he/she hold any union position?

Talking about *jobs in general* now, there are a number of things often thought important about a job. I am interested to know how important various aspects of a job are to you personally.

Listed below on this interview schedule are a number of questions about various aspects of a job. Below each question is a scale which ranges from 'Very important indeed' to 'Not at all important'. For each question please can you indicate the importance of this aspect of a job to you personally by placing an X at the appropriate point on the scale. (Show scales to respondent.)

16.   How important to you in a job is *interest and variety*?

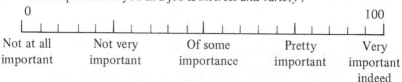

17.   How important to you in a job is the *opportunity to use skill*?[3]

18.   How important to you in a job is the opportunity to *use your own initiative and take responsibility?*

19.   How important to you in a job is *very high wages*?

20.   How important to you in a job is *security*?

21.   How important to you in a job is having *friendly, sociable and pleasant workmates*?

22.   How important to you in a job is having a *strong and active union branch*?

23.   How important to you in a job is *being able to talk to other people while you are working*?

24.   How important to you in a job is *having the feeling that the management takes an interest in you as a person*?

25.   (1) How important to you in a job is *getting along well with the foreman*?

           (2) How would the foreman have to behave for you to get along well with him?

26.   (1) Have you ever had a grievance at work?

      (If yes, ask:)

           (2) What do you do when you have a grievance at work? Always take it up with the union, usually take it up, sometimes take it up, sometimes let it go by, usually let it go by or always let it go by? (Hand prompt card.)

27.   (1) How much would you like to become a shift foreman? Very much indeed, quite a lot, not sure, not very much or not at all? (Hand prompt card.)

           (2) Why did you give that answer?

28.   How do you feel about these statements? Please can you put a tick in the appropriate box to indicate how much you agree or disagree with each statement.[4] (Show boxes to respondents.)

           (1) A firm is like a football team because good teamwork on a side means success and is to everyone's advantage.

           (2) Big business has too much power in this country.

           (3) BSC could afford to pay higher wages than it does now without damaging its prospects for the future.

           (4) Team work in industry is impossible, because employers and men are really on opposite sides.

           (5) Trade unions have too much power in this country.

29.   (1) Suppose you had a son leaving school just now, what sort of job would you like him to get?

           (2) Why did you choose that particular job?

30.   Now I would like to ask you about the jobs you held before you joined this

steelworks. (For each job held for one year or more, ask:)

(1) Please could you tell me the date you began this job and when you left?

(2) What was the name of the firm? What industry was this firm engaged in?

(3) Where was the place you worked at?

(4) What kind of job was this?

(5) Were you a trade union member when you held that job?

(6) How did you feel about trade unions in general when you held that job? Strongly approve, mildly approve, feel neither for nor against, mildly disapprove or strongly disapprove?

(7) (If respondent was a trade union member at that time, ask:) How much did you do for your branch when you held that job? A great deal, a fair amount, a little, not very much or nothing at all?

(8) How many jobs have you held altogether, including present one? (Include all jobs irrespective of time held.)

(9) (1) Have you ever been unemployed for a length of time, say longer than a month?

(If yes, ask:)

(2) How many times have you been unemployed for longer than a month? (Tape)

(3) How long did each period of unemployment last? (Tape)

(4) What do you remember about these experiences? (Tape)

Now I would like to ask you some questions about yourself and your family.

31. (1) Are you married, single, separated, divorced or widowed?

(If married or previously married, ask:)

(2) Do you have any children?

(3) Please could you tell me their names, so we can sort them out in these boxes?

(For each child, ask:)

(4) How old is he/she?

(5) (If child is over 14 and less than 19, ask:)
Is he/she still at school?

32. I would like to ask you about the occupations of the members of your family. By this I mean the occupations they have had for the major part of their life. (If kin member is unemployed or temporarily sick, ask for normal occupation. If kin member is dead, chronically sick, retired or on 'light work', ask for previous occupation. If kin member is a housewife, ask for her previous occupation, if any.)

(1) What is/was X's occupation? What industry is/was his/her job connected with?

(2) (If steelworker, ask:) Does X work/or ever worked here at (steelworks)?

(3) Is/was X a trade union member?

(4) How do you think X feels/felt about trade unions in general? Strongly approves, mildly approves, neither for nor against, mildly disapproves, strongly disapproves or don't you know? (Hand prompt card.)

(5) (If X belongs to a trade union, ask:) How much would you say X does /did for his/her branch? A great deal, a fair amount, a little, not very

much, nothing at all or don't you know? (Hand prompt card.) Does/ did X hold any union position?

33. What type of school did you last attend? Was it a Secondary Modern, Elementary or Senior, Technical, Grammar, Comprehensive, Central or Intermediate, or other?

34. How old were you when you left this school?

35. (1) Have you had any further education since leaving school?
    (If yes, ask:)
    (2) Was it full-time, part-time (day) or part-time (evening)?
    (3) For how long did you attend?

36. Do you have any qualifications? For example City and Guilds, National Ordinary Level, O levels, evening school certificates? Have you served an apprenticeship?

37. (1) Do you belong to any clubs, societies or organisations? For example a sports club, a tenant's association, a gardening club, a church, a political party, a workingman's club, a BSC club? (If yes, ask for each club name.)
    (2) How often do you go to meetings/attend services/go for a drink there/ play a game there etc.? How often in fact are meetings held/services held/club is open/can play a game etc.?
    (3) Are you on any committees?
    (4) Do you hold any official positions?

38. What do you do in your spare time? What are your hobbies and interests? For example gardening, fishing, watching television, 'do it yourself', going to the pub, camping, working on the car, dancing, football, cycling, cabinet making?

39. (1) Which of the following things did you do last week (i.e. from today to a week ago today) and how many times did you do each? (Hand prompt card.) (These were: went to the pub; went dancing; went to the cinema with someone; went out to dinner with someone; called on friend/s; had friend/s in; went to watch a match, for example a football or cricket match; played sport of some kind; went to the theatre or concert; went to a night club; went to a trade union function of some kind; went to a club or society meeting (not trade union); went to a party; went to a workingman's club; went to church; went shopping with the wife (if applicable); took the children to do or see something (if applicable).) Did you take part in any other activity not mentioned on the card? How many times did you do this?
    (2) Which shift/s were you on last week? Did you work over the weekend?

40. How much of the time do you enjoy being with other people – aside from your family I mean? A great deal of the time, quite a bit of the time, some- times like to be with other people, sometimes prefer to be on your own or just with the family, quite often like to be on your own or just with the family or really like to be on your own or just with the family most of the time? (Hand prompt card.)

41. Who do you most often spend your spare time with? (Point out that re- latives other than wives, children or other relatives living in the same house

as the respondent can be included.)

(1) Please could you give me just their first names, so that we can sort them out in these boxes?

(Ask for each person named)

(2) What is X's occupation? What industry is his job connected with? (Classify wives by husband's occupation.)

(3) (If steelworker, ask:) Does X work here at this steelworks?

(4) Is X a trade union member?

(5) How do you think X feels about trade unions in general? Strongly approves, mildly approves, neither for nor against, mildly disapproves, strongly disapproves, or don't you know? (Hand prompt card.)

(6) (If X belongs to a trade union, ask:) How much would you say X does for his/her branch? A great deal, a fair amount, a little, not very much, nothing at all or don't you know? (Hand prompt card.) Does X hold any union position?

Now I would like to ask you some questions about where you live.

42.   What is your address? (Explain to respondent that this is needed to see which areas of Sheffield/Rotherham respondents tend to live in.)

43.   Do you own your home or do you rent it? (If respondent rents it, ask:) Whom do you rent it from? (If respondent lives with parents, ask if parents own or rent it.)

44.   What kind of home do you have? Is it a flat, detached house, semi-detached house, terraced house or other kind of home?

45.   When roughly was your home built?

46.   How long have you lived there?

47.   How much do you see socially of the people in your neighbourhood? A great deal, quite a lot, to some extent, not a great deal, not at all or don't you live near anyone? (Hand prompt card.)

48.   Now I would like to ask you some questions about your next-door neighbours (i.e. the people living next-door and next-door-but-one on both sides of your own house, or nearest equivalent).

(For each set of neighbours, ask:)

(1) How well do you know the people living in this house? Very well, quite well, a little, not very well, not at all? (Hand prompt card.)

(2) What is the occupation of X (referring to the head of the household)? What industry is his job connected with?

(3) (If steelworker, ask:) Does X work here at this steelworks?

(If neighbours known very well or quite well ask:)

(4) Is X a trade union member?

(5) How do you think X feels about trade unions in general? Strongly approves, mildly approves, neither for nor against, mildly disapproves, strongly disapproves, or don't you know? (Hand prompt card.)

(If X is a trade union member, ask:)

(6) How much would you say X does for his/her branch? A great deal, a fair amount, a little, not very much, nothing at all or don't you know? (Hand prompt card.) Does X hold any union position?

49. (1) Where did you live for most of your childhood and youth? What kind of area was that?

(2) (If urban area, ask:) Did most people own or rent their homes there? (If rented, ask:) Who did they rent their homes from?

(3) What kind of jobs did people living there have?

(4) How many homes have you had altogether including your present one? (Only count homes lived in for at least one year.)

Now I would like to ask you some questions about trade unions. (Explain to respondent that his answers to some of these questions will be tape-recorded. Assure him again of confidentiality; point out that only his code number will be recorded on tape-recorder, not his name.)

50. When did you first join a trade union?

51. Why did you first join a trade union? (Tape)

Actives only

52. (1) How did you first become active in a trade union branch? (Tape)

(2) And why do you continue to be active in your branch now? (Tape)

53. Why do you think some people don't take an active part in the branch? (Tape)

54. (1) Would you like a full-time union job? (Tape)

(2) Why would you like/dislike a full-time union job? (Tape)

Inactives only

55. Is there any particular reason why you don't take a very active part in the branch? (Tape)

56. (1) Would you like to be on the branch committee or a branch official? (Tape)

(2) (If no, ask:) Is there any particular reason why you wouldn't like to (Tape)

57. Why do you think some people do take an active part in the branch? (Tape)

All

58. (1) What part do you think trade unions should play in British industrial life? A very important part, a pretty important part, a part of some importance, only a small part, no part at all or don't you know?

(2) (If a small part or larger, ask:) What do you think trade unions in general and your own branch in particular should try to achieve in the industrial area? (Tape)

(3) Some people say trade unions should just be concerned with getting higher pay and better conditions for their members. Others think they should also try to get workers a say in management. Which do you agree with?

59. (1) What part do you think trade unions should play in British political life? A very important part, a pretty important part, a part of some importance, only a small part, no part at all or don't you know?

(2) (If a small part or larger, ask:) What do you think trade unions should try to achieve in the political area? (Tape)

(3) As you know, most trade unions support the Labour Party; do you approve of this or do you think they ought to keep themselves separate?

60. (1) What part do you think trade unions should play in workers' social lives? A very important part, a pretty important part, a part of some importance, only a small part, no part at all or don't you know?

(2) (If a small part or larger, ask:) What do you think trade unions should try to provide in workers' social lives? (Tape)

61. How do you feel about strikes? Which of these three statements do you agree with most: I would go on strike if the union called one but I personally wouldn't want to; I would willingly go on strike if the union called one which I considered necessary; I would go on strike if I considered it necessary whether or not the union approved?

62. How do you feel about going on strike in support of workers at other plants? (Tape)

63. (1) Have you ever been on strike?
(If yes, ask:)
(2) How many times have you been on strike? (Tape)
(3) How long did each strike last? (Tape)
(4) Do you particularly remember any of these strikes? (Tape)

64. (1) Do you remember your father ever being on strike?
(2) (If yes, ask:) Can you tell me about it? How did he feel about it? (Tape)

65. (1) Do you remember your father ever being unemployed for any length of time?
(2) (If yes, ask:) Can you tell me about it? How did he feel about it? (Tape)

66. (1) If a branch official accepted promotion to shift foreman, how would you feel about it? Strongly approve, mildly approve, have no feelings either way, mildly disapprove, strongly disapprove or don't you know?
(2) Why would you feel this way? (Tape)

67. (1) Would you say you were *close friends* with any of the officials or committee men in your branch?
(2) (If yes, ask:) Which ones are these?

Actives only
(3) Did you get to know X before or after you yourself first became active?

68. How easy is it for you to get to branch meetings in terms of travelling there? Very easy, fairly easy, so-so, fairly difficult or very difficult?

69. (1) Do you pay Labour Party dues?
(2) (If no, ask:) Have you contracted out then?

70. How much would you say you discussed politics? A very great deal, quite a lot, now and then, not very much or not at all.

71. (1) How did you vote in the last few general elections (i.e. 1959, 1964, 1966 and 1970)?
(2) (If no change from 1959 or earliest vote, ask:) Why do you vote for that particular Party? (Tape)
(3) OR (If respondent has changed voting pattern at all, ask:) Why did you change your vote in this way? (Tape)

108

72.   People often talk about there being different social classes – what do you think? (Tape)

Points to try and cover in general discussion, no specified order
(*Try and obtain an answer for these questions even if the respondent considers that there are no classes today.)
(1)   Number of major social classes in present day society.
(2)   Names of these.
(3)   Major factor(s) used to determine class position of individuals and groups. Reasons why individuals and groups hold their particular positions. (Look for position of white-collar workers relative to manual workers.)
(4)   Own class.
(5)   Amount of class conflict, reasons for its existence. The general relationship between men and management in society.
(6)   Extent of upward social mobility possible.
*(7)   Past and future social change, possibility and direction of.
*(8)   Role of trade unions in past and future social change. Nature of the future social change trade unions will be involved in.
*(9)   Satisfaction with present-day society. Improvements, reforms or radical changes desired. The necessity and desirability of the class system.

APPENDIX 3
SURVEY FINDINGS ON SELECTED ASPECTS

Notes on tables

(1)   To assess the attitude towards trade unions of respondents' adult children, workmates, leisure-time companions, siblings, fathers and wives, the respondent was asked for each person in turn 'How do you think X feels (or felt) about trade unions in general?'. He was then handed a card on which were provided six categories of approval ranging from 'strongly approves' to 'strongly disapproves' including a 'don't know' category, and asked to choose the reply most suited to the attitude of the person in question.

(2)   To assess the amount of branch activity of respondents' adult children (full-time students were included here), leisure-time companions, siblings, fathers and wives, the respondent was asked, for each person in turn, if that person was a trade union member, 'How much would you say X does (or did) for his/her branch?'. He was then handed a card giving six categories of participation ranging from 'a great deal' to 'nothing at all' again including a 'don't know' category and asked to choose the most appropriate.

(3)   To assess the amount of branch activity of respondents' workmates (who were all members of the two steelworks shops) the total scores from the participation questionnaire survey were utilised. The participation scores were divided into five groups as follows.

Participation score	*Amount of activity undertaken in branch*
Over 13	'A great deal'
11, 12	'A fair amount'
8, 9, 10	'A little'
6, 7	'Not very much'
under 5	'Nothing at all'

In the case of workfriends named by the respondents who had chosen not to fill in the participation questionnaire, the two branch secretaries' ratings of the amount of activity these persons undertook in branch affairs were used; see above (Appendix 1).

(4)   To assess the type of enumeration district in which the respondent currently lived, the respondent was asked in the interview for his address, including his house number. (If the respondent had lived at that address for less than a year he was asked for information on his previous address.) The respondents' present addresses were looked up on a map of the Sheffield/Rotherham area showing the 1966 (ten percent) Census Enumeration Districts and a note made of the relevant Enumeration District numbers. These Enumeration Districts were then classified according to the pre-

dominant type of tenure (council, rented, owner-occupied, mixed) and, according to their social class composition, into eight groups. (For use of this method, I am indebted to Balwin, T., and Bottoms, A.E., *The Urban Criminal* (London, Tavistock Publication, 1975)). These were:

1.   Council rough – where more than ⅓ of the residents were in the Registrar General's classes IV and V.
2.   Council respectable – where less than ⅓ of the residents were in the Registrar General's classes IV and V.
3.   Rented rough – where more than ⅓ of the residents were in the Registrar General's classes IV and V.
4.   Rented respectable – where less than ⅓ of the residents were in the Registrar General's classes IV and V.
5.   Owner-occupied select – where more than ⅓ of the residents were in the Registrar General's classes I and II.
6.   Owner-occupied not select – where less than ⅓ of the residents were in the Registrar General's classes I and II.
7.   Mixed rough – where no one kind of tenure predominated, and more than ⅓ were in the Registrar General's classes IV and V.
8.   Mixed respectable – where no one kind of tenure predominated, and less than ⅓ of the residents were in the Registrar General's classes IV and V.

To assess the type of enumeration district in which the respondent spent his childhood and youth, he was asked to describe the area in terms of the mode of tenure and the social class composition of its inhabitants. The types of districts described by the respondents were first of all divided into two basic groups: those located in the urban areas of cities and large towns; and those located in rural areas, villages or small towns. Within this basic classification, the districts were further subdivided. In the case of the first group, into eight subgroups classified according to the type of tenure predominant in the area and the social class composition of the residents, in the same way as the respondents' present areas of residence were classified. In the case of the second group, they were classified into rural areas including agricultural villages, industrial villages, and small industrial towns.

(5)   The following table shows the occupational classification used for analysing the material on the occupations of respondents' kin, leisure-time companions and that on respondents' own previous occupations, adapted from Goldthorpe *et al.* (1968A, pp. 196–7).

Occupational classification[a]

Occupational status level	Examples	Summary classifications used in text
1(a) Higher professional, managerial and other white-collar employees	Lawyer, graduate teacher, doctor	Non-manual or white collar
(b) Large industrial or commercial employers. Landed proprieters	–	

Occupational classification (cont.)

Occupational status level	Examples	Summary classifications used in text
2(a) Intermediate professional, management and other white-collar employees	Non-graduate teacher, nurse, departmental manager	Non-manual or white-collar
(b) Medium industrial or commercial employers, substantial farmers	–	
3(a) Lower professional, managerial and other white-collar employees	Laboratory assistant, sales representative, computer operator, professional sportsman	
(b) Small industrial or commercial employers, small proprietors, small farmers	Jobbing builder, driving instructor, grocer, post office mistress	
4(a) Supervisory, inspectional, minor officials and other white-collar employees	Mining deputy, foreman, shop assistant, petrol pump attendant, policeman	Intermediate
(b) Self-employed man (no employees or expensive capital equipment)	Steel erector, window cleaner	
5 Skilled manual workers (with apprenticeship or equivalent)	Post Office engineer, bricklayer	Manual
6 Other relatively skilled manual workers	Steelworkers, miners, cotton workers, painters and decorators	
7 Semi-skilled manual workers	Cutlery buffer	
8 Unskilled manual workers	Farm labourer, builder's labourer, dustman, cleaner	

[a] If the kin member or companion was unemployed or temporarily sick, his normal occupation was taken. If he/she was dead, chronically sick, retired or on 'light work', the previous occupation was taken. If she was a housewife, her previous occupation if any was taken, and if he/she was a university or college student, he/she was classified as non-manual.

Table A3.1   *Respondents' marital status*

Marital status	Inactive %	Active %
(1) Married	76.3	95.5
(2) Separated, divorced, widowed	8.5	0
(3) Single	15.3	4.5
Total	100 ($N = 59$)	100 ($N = 66$)

Note: 1-tailed X^2 test (1) $v.$ (2) + (3) P = 0.001, θ = 0.41

Table A3.2 Survey information on characteristics of their children for those respondents presently or previously married

	(i)		(ii)		(iii)		(iv)		(v)		(vi)		(vii)		(viii)		(ix)	
	Number of children in total		Number of dependent children				For those respondents with one or more children at work						Number of children who 'strongly approve' of trade unions[a]		Number of children belonging to a trade union[a]		Number of children belonging to a trade union who undertake a 'great deal', a 'fair amount' or a 'little' branch activity[a]	
			Respondents aged under 40 years		Respondents aged 40 years or more		Number of children with intermediate occupations		Number of children with non-manual occupations		Number of children working in the steel industry							
Number of children	Inactive %	Active %	Inactive %	Active %	Inactive %	Active %	Inactive %	Active %	Inactive %	Active %	Inactive %	Active %	Inactive %	Active %	Inactive %	Active %	Inactive %	Active %
0	20.0	6.3	21.7	9.1	48.1	53.7	72.7	46.9	77.3	71.9	86.4	78.1	90.9	51.5	40.9	45.4	92.3	50.0
1	26.0	19.0	34.8	13.6	22.2	26.8	22.7	34.4	13.6	25.0	13.6	12.5	9.1	33.3	59.1	36.4	7.7	38.9
2	28.0	27.0	21.7	22.7	14.8	12.2	4.5	15.6	4.5	0	0	6.2	0	6.1	0	9.1	0	5.6
3	12.0	27.0	13.0	40.9	7.4	2.4	0	3.1	4.5	3.1	0	3.1	0	9.1	0	9.1	0	5.6
4	6.0	9.5	8.7	13.6	7.4	4.9												
5 or more	8.0	11.1																
Total	100 (N=50)	100 (N=63)	100 (N=23)	100 (N=22)	100 (N=27)	100 (N=41)	100 (N=22)	100 (N=32)	100 (N=22)	100 (N=32)	100 (N=22)	100 (N=32)	100 (N=22)	100 (N=33)	100 (N=22)	100 (N=33)	100 (N=13)	100 (N=18)

Notes:
Column (i)   K–S test P = 0.10, G = 0.31.
Column (ii)   1-tailed K–S test P = 0.10, G = 0.47.
Column (iii)   1-tailed K–S test P > 0.10.
Column (vii)   1-tailed K–S test, P = 0.05, G = 0.81.
Column (ix)   Fisher's Exact Test with prediction, 0 v. 1 or more P = 0.07, G = 0.85.

[a] includes one full-time student.

Table A3.3 *Survey information on characteristics of respondents' workmates considered to be 'close friends'*

Number of workmates	(i) Number of workmates named as 'close friends' Inactive %	(i) Active %	(ii) Number of workmate close friends seen outside work Inactive %	(ii) Active %	(iii) All respondents Inactive %	(iii) Active %	(iv) Respondents aged under 40 years Inactive %	(iv) Active %	(v) Respondents aged 40 years or more Inactive %	(v) Active %	(vi) All respondents Inactive %	(vi) Active %	(vii) Respondents aged under 40 years Inactive %	(vii) Active %	(viii) Respondents aged 40 years or more Inactive %	(viii) Active %
					For those respondents with at least one workmate 'close friend' — Number of workmate 'close friends' who 'strongly approve' of trade unions						Number of workmate 'close friends' undertaking a 'great deal' or a 'fair amount' of branch activity					
0	61.0	43.9	4.3	16.2	69.6	37.8	85.7	42.9	44.4	34.8	60.9	32.4	71.4	14.3	44.4	43.5
1	11.9	18.2	39.1	27.0	21.7	32.4	7.1	28.6	44.4	34.8	30.4	32.4	21.4	28.6	44.4	34.8
2	6.8	12.1	13.0	24.3	8.7	8.1	7.1	7.1	11.1	8.7	8.7	10.8	7.1	14.3	11.1	8.7
3	8.5	10.6	21.7	16.2		2.7	0	7.1	0	0	0	16.2	0	35.7	0	4.3
4	8.5	4.5	17.4	8.1	} 0	} 18.9	} 0	} 14.3	} 0	} 21.7	} 0	} 8.1	} 0	} 7.1	} 0	} 8.7
5	1.7	6.1	4.3	2.7												
6 or more	1.7	4.5	0	5.4												
Total	100 (N=59)	100 (N=66)	100 (N=23)	100 (N=37)	100 (N=23)	100 (N=37)	100 (N=14)	100 (N=14)	100 (N=9)	100 (N=23)	100 (N=23)	100 (N=37)	100 (N=14)	100 (N=14)	100 (N=9)	100 (N=23)

Notes:

Column (i)	1-tailed K–S test P = 0.10, G = 0.24.
Column (ii)	1-tailed K–S test P > 0.10.
Column (iii)	1-tailed K–S test P = 0.10, G = 0.57.
Column (iv)	1-tailed K–S test P = 0.10, G = 0.73.
Column (v)	1-tailed K–S test P > 0.10.
Column (vi)	1-tailed K–S test P = 0.10, G = 0.55.
Column (vii)	1-tailed K–S test P = 0.05, G = 0.85.
Column (viii)	1-tailed K–S test P > 0.10.

Table A3.4   *Types of social activity undertaken by respondents one or more times during the week preceding the interview*

Type of social activity	Inactive %		Active %	
Went to a pub	69.5		58.5	
Went to a working man's club	50.8		52.3	
Called on somebody	40.7		46.2	
Had somebody in	35.6		33.8	
Went to watch a match of some kind	8.5		30.8	
Played sport of some kind	5.1		9.2	
Went to betting shop/dog track	3.4		1.5	
Went fishing in company of other/s	6.8		7.7	
Went dancing or to a night club	8.5	(*N*=59)	10.8	(*N*=65[a])
Went to a theatre or concert	3.4		0	
Went to the cinema	6.8		4.6	
Went to a club or society meeting	1.7		12.3	
Went to a trade union function of some kind	1.7		13.8	
Went to an evening class	0		3.1	
Went to church	5.1		1.5	
Went out to dinner or to a party	6.8		20.0	
Other (e.g. wedding, motoring outing)	3.4		1.5	
Went shopping with the wife	51.1	(*N*=45)	49.2	(*N*=63)
Took the children to do or see something	21.9	(*N*=32)	51.3	(*N*=39)

[a] 1 respondent was on holiday during the week preceding the interview and therefore was omitted.

Table A3.5   *Respondents' hobbies and spare-time interests*

Type of hobby/spare time interest	Inactive %	Active %
(1) Gardening	50.8	50.0
(2) Working on the car	28.8	30.3
(3) Watching television	28.8	24.2
(4) Following football	27.1	31.8
(5) Do-it-yourself	27.1	27.3
(6) Going to the pub	28.8	21.2
(7) Playing sport of some kind[a]	15.3	37.9
(8) Fishing	18.6	24.2
(9) Motoring	5.1	16.7
(10) Going to working men's club	10.2	9.1
(11) Dancing	6.8	9.1
(12) Reading	5.1	12.1
(13) Gambling	8.5	6.1
(14) Other	37.3	51.5
	(*N*=59)	(*N*=66)

[a] Row (7) 1-tailed X^2 test P = 0.005, G = 0.29.

Table A3.6 Survey findings on characteristics of respondents' leisure-time companions

Number of companions	(i) Number of persons named in total		(ii) Number of companions with intermediate occupations		(iii) Number of companions with non-manual occupations		(iv) Number of companions working in the steel industry		(v) Number of companions who are also 'workmates'		(vi) Number of companions of trade unions — All respondents		(vii) Respondents aged under 40 years		(viii) Respondents aged 40 years or more		(ix) Number of companions belonging to a trade union		(x) Number of companions belonging to a trade union who undertake a 'great deal' or a 'fair amount' of branch activity — All respondents		(xi) Respondents aged under 40 years		(xii) Respondents aged 40 years or more	
	Inactive %	Active %	Inactive %	Active %	Inactive %	Active %	Inactive %	Active %	Inactive %	Active %	Inactive %	Active %	Inactive %	Active %	Inactive %	Active %	Inactive %	Active %	Inactive %	Active %	Inactive %	Active %	Inactive %	Active %
0	20.3	19.7	72.3	79.2	74.5	56.6	40.4	28.3	78.7	62.3	68.1	30.2	84.0	15.0	50.0	39.4	21.3	15.1	86.5	42.2	85.0	30.0	88.2	52.0
1	22.0	10.6	23.4	15.1	14.9	22.6	38.3	34.0	14.9	24.5	27.7	32.1	16.0	50.0	40.9	21.2	34.0	32.1	13.5	33.3	15.0	40.0	11.8	28.0
2	18.6	16.7	2.1	5.7	6.4	9.4	8.5	24.5	4.3	7.5	4.3	11.3	0	10.0	9.1	12.1	27.7	22.6	0	13.3	0	20.0	0	8.0
3	5.1	9.1	2.1	0	2.1	1.9	6.4	5.7	2.1	1.9	0	7.5	0	5.0	0	4.1	4.3	7.5	0	4.4	0	5.0	0	4.0
4	15.2	22.7	} 0	} 0	2.1	5.7	4.3	1.9	} 0	} 3.8	0	7.5	} 0	15.0	0	3.0	4.3	9.4	} 0	} 6.7	} 0	} 5.0	0	0
5	1.7	3.0			} 0	} 3.8	} 2.1	} 5.7			0	7.5		} 5.0	0	} 15.2	4.3	1.9					} 0	} 8.0
6	5.1	6.1									} 0	} 11.3			} 0		} 4.3	} 11.3						
7 or more	11.9	12.1																						
Total	100 (N=59)	100 (N=66)	100 (N=47)	100 (N=53)	100 (N=47)	100 (N=53)	100 (N=47)	100 (N=53)	100 (N=47)	100 (N=53)	100 (N=47)	100 (N=53)	100 (N=25)	100 (N=20)	100 (N=22)	100 (N=33)	100 (N=47)	100 (N=53)	100 (N=37)	100 (N=45)	100 (N=20)	100 (N=20)	100 (N=17)	100 (N=25)

Notes:
Column (i)   1-tailed K–S test P > 0.10.
Column (vi)   1-tailed K–S test P = 0.001, G = 0.62
Column (vii) 1-tailed K–S test P = 0.001, G = 0.94
Column (viii) 1-tailed K–S test P = 0.10, G = 0.39
Column (x)   1-tailed K–S test P = 0.001, G = 0.81
Column (xi)   1-tailed K–S test P = 0.001, G = 0.87
Column (xii) 1-tailed K–S test P = 0.10, G = 0.76

116

Table A3.7   Survey findings on characteristics of siblings for respondents possessing one or more

Number of siblings	(i) Number of siblings with intermediate occupations		(ii) Number of siblings with non-manual occupations		(iii) Number of siblings who 'strongly approve' of trade unions		(iv) Number of siblings belonging to a trade union		(v) Number of siblings belonging to a trade union who undertake a 'great deal' or a 'fair amount' of branch activity	
	Inactive %	Active %	Inactive %	Active %	Inactive %	Active %	Inactive %	Active %	Inactive %	Active %
0	65.5	72.6	60.0	59.7	70.9	41.9	34.5	22.6	83.3	54.2
1	32.7	24.2	30.9	25.8	18.2	37.1	36.4	38.7	11.1	29.2
2	0	1.6	5.5	6.5	5.5	12.9	14.5	21.0	2.8	14.6
3 or more	1.8	0	3.6	6.5	5.5	8.1	14.5	17.7	2.8	2.1
Don't know	0	1.6	0	1.6	0	0	0	0	0	0
Total	100 (N=55)	100 (N=62)	100 (N=55)	100 (N=62)	100 (N=55)	100 (N=62)	100 (N=55)	100 (N=62)	100 (N=36)	100 (N=48)

Notes: Column (iii) 1-tailed K–S test $P = 0.01$, $G = 0.43$.
Column (v) 1-tailed K–S test $P = 0.05$, $G = 0.57$.

Table A3.8 *Survey findings on characteristics of respondents' fathers*

(i) Fathers' occupations

	Inactive %	Active %
Manual	86.4	89.4
Intermediate	6.8	4.5
Non-manual	6.8	4.5
Don't know	0	1.5
Total	100 (N=59)	100 (N=66)

(ii) Fathers' trade-union attitudes

	Inactive %	Active %
(1) Strongly approves	28.8	48.5
(2) Mildly approves	13.6	18.2
(3) Neither for nor against	10.2	6.1
(4) Mildly disapproves	0	0
(5) Strongly disapproves	3.4	6.1
(6) Don't know	44.1	21.2
Total	100 (N=59)	100 (N=66)

(iii) Fathers' trade-union membership

	Inactive %	Active %
Member	71.2	72.7
Not a member	22.0	22.7
Don't know	6.8	4.5
Total	100 (N=59)	100 (N=66)

(iv) Fathers' branch activity for those who are trade union members

	Inactive %	Active %
(1) Great deal	14.3	22.9
(2) Fair amount	7.1	18.8
(3) A little	2.4	12.5
(4) Not very much	4.8	8.3
(5) Nothing at all	50.0	35.4
(6) Don't know	21.4	2.1
Total	100 (N=42)	100 (N=48)

Notes: Column (ii) 1-tailed X^2 test (1) $v.$ (2) to (6) P = 0.05, G = 0.40.
Column (iv) 1-tailed X^2 test (1) + (2) $v.$ (3) to (6) P = 0.05, G = 0.45.

Table A3.9 *Survey findings on characteristics of respondents' wives for those presently or previously married*

	(i) Wives' occupations (past or present)		(ii) Wives' trade union attitudes			(iii) Wives' trade union membership (past or present)			(iv) Wives' branch activity for those who are/were trade union members		
	Inactive %	Active %		Inactive %	Active %		Inactive %	Active %		Inactive %	Active %
Manual	50.0	52.4	(1) Strongly approves	10.0	30.2	(1) Member	30.0	52.4	(1) Great deal	0	3.6
Intermediate	18.0	19.0	(2) Mildly approves	12.0	15.9	(2) Not a member	66.0	44.4	(2) Fair amount	0	3.6
Non-manual	26.0	27.0	(3) Neither for nor against	34.0	38.1	(3) Don't know	4.0	3.2	(3) A little	13.3	32.1
None	6.0	1.6	(4) Mildly disapproves	4.0	4.8				(4) Not very much	0	3.6
			(5) Strongly disapproves	6.0	0				(5) Nothing at all	80.0	46.4
			(6) Don't know	34.0	11.1				(6) Don't know	6.7	10.7
Total	100 (N=50)	100 (N=63)	Total	100 (N=50)	100 (N=63)	Total	100 (N=50)	100 (N=63)	Total	100 (N=15)	100 (N=28)

Notes: Column (ii) 1-tailed X^2 test (1) v. (2) to (6) P = 0.01, G = 0.57.
Column (iii) 1-tailed X^2 test (1) v. (2) + (3) P = 0.10, G = 0.30.
Column (iv) 1-tailed X^2 test (1) to (3) v. (4) to (6) P = 0.10, G = 0.62.

Table A3.10 Survey findings on the type of enumeration districts respondents presently lived in and those in which they spent their childhood and youth

		(i) Type of district respondents presently live in in Sheffield/Rotherham conurbation		(ii) Type of district respondents spent childhood and youth in — All respondents		(iii) Respondents aged under 40 years		(iv) Respondents aged 40 years or more	
		Inactive %	Active %	Inactive %	Active %	Inactive %	Active %	Inactive %	Active %
(1) Council rough	located in city or large town	33.9	24.2	15.5	13.6	26.7	29.2	3.6	4.8
(2) Council respectable		15.3	28.8	1.7	0	0	0	3.6	0
(3) Rented rough		15.3	15.2	32.8	51.5	33.3	37.5	32.1	59.5
(4) Rented respectable		1.7	4.5	8.6	6.1	3.3	8.3	14.3	4.8
(5) Owner-occupied select		3.4	4.5	0	0	0	0	0	0
(6) Owner-occupied not select		23.7	13.6	15.5	7.6	23.3	4.2	7.1	9.5
(7) Mixed rough		3.4	1.5	3.4	0	6.7	0	0	0
(8) Mixed respectable		3.4	7.6	0	1.5	0	4.2	0	0
(9) Small industrial town		N/A	N/A	6.9	1.5	0	0	14.3	2.4
(10) Industrial village (mainly mining)		N/A	N/A	10.3	13.6	3.3	16.7	17.9	11.9
(11) Rural area (including agricultural villages)		N/A	N/A	5.2	4.5	3.3	0	7.1	7.1
Total		100 (N=59)	100 (N=66)	100 (N=58^a)	100 (N=66)	100 (N=30^a)	100 (N=24)	100 (N=28)	100 (N=42)

Notes: Column (ii) X^2 test (3) v. (1) + (2) + (4) to (11) P = 0.10, θ = 0.19.
Column (iii) X^2 test (3) v. (1) + (2) + (4) to (11) P > 0.10.
Column (iv) X^2 test (3) v. (1) + (2) + (4) to (11) P = 0.05, θ = 0.26.

^{a} No information one respondent.

APPENDIX 4
STATISTICAL TECHNIQUES USED IN THE ANALYSIS OF THE SURVEYS

All of the survey results were tested for significance using the Chi-square Test (X^2), the Kolmogorov-Smirnov (K-S) Test or Fisher's Exact Test.[1] Significance levels of 0.05 or less are referred to in the text as 'significant' and significance levels ranging from 0.10 to 0.055 are referred to as 'suggestive'. The significance levels are always given either directly underneath the table they refer to or, if the data are presented in the text, in a footnote. Where the data are being tested to see if they conform to the prediction of *one* particular hypothesis, a one-tailed test of significance is used. Where the data are being tested to see which of the several different predictions of two or more hypotheses they conform to, or where no particular prediction has been made in the literature as to the direction of the results, a two-tailed test is used.

Degrees of association were only calculated for relationships between variables that had been previously shown to be *suggestive* or *significant*. Measures of association used were Guttman's Coefficient of Predictability (Ga) in the case of two nominal scales;[2] the Wilcoxon Model for Nominal-Ordinal Association (θ);[3] and Goodman and Kruskal's Coefficient of Ordinal Assocation (G).[4]

APPENDIX 5
SOCIAL IMAGERY METHODOLOGY

A deliberately vague introductory question was used: the respondent was asked 'People often talk about there being different social classes – what do you think?'[1] The respondent's reply was used as the starting point for a general and relatively unstructured discussion of class. I wanted to collect information on a number of specific issues here, a check-list of which was printed on the interview schedule. But the order in which issues were raised could be varied following the natural flow of the discussion, and the questions asked of the respondents were formulated in ways consistent with what had already been learnt about the respondent's ideas and conceptions; this part of the interview was tape-recorded. If the respondent initially replied that there were no classes in society today, I still tried to establish his views on the items concerned with respondent's views on past and future social change, the role of trade unions in such social change and his satisfaction with present day society.

I adopted Cousins and Brown's system for the classification of the raw data on images of society yielded by the interview discussions.[2] Although it can be argued that these authors do not, in their study of shipbuilding workers, generally show workers with the same type of image to hold coherent sets of attitudes, they do provide a practical and logical method of classification in a very difficult and problematic area.[3] This area of research is particularly difficult, both on account of the diversity of the respondents' answers to questions on class and class differences, and because one cannot assume that each respondent has one clear image of society which provides a reference point no matter what the question.

In the initial stage of the analysis of the respondents' images, two factors were emphasised: the number and, more particularly, the types of grouping distinguished; and the respondent's own self-ranking within such a hierarchy. Relatively little attention was paid to the descriptive labels which were used by the respondents, often in very different ways. However, in the second stage of the analysis, an attempt was made to characterise the classes distinguished in terms of the actual social groups the respondents saw as constituting each class. The findings for the group of steelworkers as a whole are of considerable interest in themselves and are discussed briefly below.

I was able to distinguish in the survey, similarly to Cousins and Brown, five basic patterns or types of images from the respondents' replies, excluding ten respondents who considered that there were no classes in society today, and a further four who had no communicable image. These basic patterns are illustrated diagrammatically in Figure A5.1; Table A5.1 gives the composition in terms of actual social groups of the classes specified by the respondents.

Fig. A5.1   *Types of social image held by respondents*

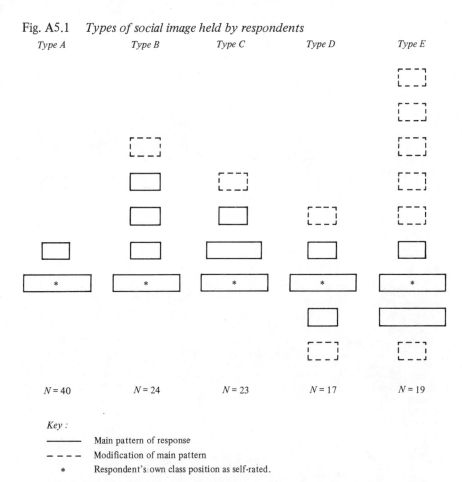

Type A	Type B	Type C	Type D	Type E
N = 40	N = 24	N = 23	N = 17	N = 19

Key :

—————— Main pattern of response

– – – – Modification of main pattern

＊   Respondent's own class position as self-rated.

It was found that nearly a third (40) out of the 123 respondents with communicable images of society distinguished two groups: the class to which they, and by inference or explicitly, most other people (including all manual workers and white-collar workers) belonged; and a relatively much smaller group containing people such as employers and directors (the 'bosses'), 'the rich', property-owners, managers and/or other similar elite groups (Type A).

Smaller proportions of the respondents, of the order of 14 to 19 per cent, possessed social images conforming to the other four types. Nineteen per cent (24) also conceived of their own class position as a member of a large grouping to which, by inference or explicitly, most people belonged (including this time, foremen as well), but were prepared to distinguish two, three or four small superior groups (Type B). These groups or 'classes' were made up, as in the case of Type A, of 'bosses', 'the rich', property-owners and managers, but also included were royalty, aristocracy, gentry and 'those with titles' ('nobs') and professionals.

The third type of pattern (Type C) was also held by 19 per cent (23) of the respondents with communicable images. Here the respondents also saw themselves as members of a large class at the bottom of the hierarchy, but in addition they distinguished a relatively large superior class of white-collar workers and well-paid or

Table A5.1 *Composition of classes and type of image of class structure in respondents' social imagery*

	Type A %	Type B %	Type C %	Type D %	Type E %
Elite group(s)					
Bosses	32	38	39	24	37
Rich	22	42	26	24	21
Nobs	12	33	13	6	32
Property owners	28	33	8	18	16
Professionals	18	42	0	0	16
Managers	30	29	17	29	26
Small businessmen	5	17	4	24	10
Large superior class					
White-collar workers			83		
Well-off workers			26		
Professionals			17		
Managers			17		
Small businessmen			13		
Own class					
Workers	88	88	87	71	21
Well-paid workers	0	0	17	18	74
White-collar workers	85	88	13	71	84
Foremen	30	67	30	35	37
Inferior class(es)					
Low-paid workers				0	79
Unemployed				41	26
Scroungers				29	21
Old age pensioners				18	0
Total	$N = 40$	$N = 24$	$N = 23$	$N = 17$	$N = 19$

skilled workers, as well as enumerating (except in two cases) one or two elite groups. These were similar to the groups distinguished by the other types and they consisted predominantly of 'bosses' and 'the rich'.

The remainder of the respondents saw themselves as members of some sort of class in an intermediate position in the hierarchy, with groups above and below them. They can be subdivided into two: 14 per cent (17) who distinguished one or two relatively small inferior groups of the unemployed, 'scroungers' or old age pensioners (Type D); and 15 per cent (19) who distinguished a relatively large inferior class of low-paid, unskilled workers. Some of the latter respondents also distinguished, in addition, a smaller inferior group below the large inferior class. All of these respondents enumerated at least one (and in one case six) smaller elite group superior to themselves consisting of 'bosses', 'the rich', 'nobs', managers and/or small businessmen.

The factors or criteria used by individuals to distinguish between classes were not involved in the basic classification of images into types, which was already complicated enough. Nevertheless, these factors are particularly important, according to Cousins and Brown, because it can be argued that they can greatly affect the interpretation to be placed on any classification of images of society.[4] They quote, as an example, the case of Goldthorpe *et al.*'s study of 'the affluent worker', where it was suggested that the emphasis on money as a determinant of class was crucially important, enabling the majority of the Luton respondents (many of whom Cousins and Brown consider to have had images of society not unlike those of their own respondents) to be classified as having a pecuniary model of the class structure. However, Cousins and Brown in their study of shipbuilding workers, and Platt in her re-examination of some of the 'affluent worker' data, found that respondents did not make, or did not grasp, the distinction between *determinants* and *correlates* of class.[5] Thus Cousins and Brown argue that references to income, wealth, and standard of living should be judged with great caution as indicating a 'money model' of the class structure and appear more likely to indicate a convenient way of referring briefly to the whole range of social differences of which 'money' is a symbol. Thus, in their own survey they found that, although four-fifths of the sample referred to 'money' as a criterion for distinguishing between classes – by far the most frequently mentioned item – only a fifth did not also make reference to one or more other criteria.

Similarly in this study of steelworkers, it was found that, whereas well over half the respondents (72 out of 123 – 58 per cent) referred to 'money' as a criterion, only 13 out of 123 (11 per cent) referred to it as the sole criterion. Accordingly it was *not* concluded here that these steelworkers had predominantly pecuniary images of society. Other criteria which were mentioned by the respondents, in conjunction with money, were behaviour and style of life (37 out of 123 – 30 per cent), background and birth (43 out of 123 – 35 per cent), occupation (34 out of 123 – 28 per cent) and property or business ownership (40 out of 123 – 32 per cent).

APPENDIX 6

CLASSIFICATION OF FORMAL ASSOCIATIONS

Nature of functions	Probable composition of membership in terms of occupational status[a]		
	Predominantly white-collar	Mixed	Predominantly manual
Diffuse	Freemasons	Old comrades' clubs Buffaloes	Working men's clubs Social clubs (similar to above) British Legion clubs
Intermediate	Tennis clubs Golf clubs	BSC social club Labour Party	Darts clubs Fishing clubs Pigeon clubs
Specific	Parachute clubs	BSC's sports clubs Gardening clubs Photography clubs	Bingo clubs Tenants' associations

[a] Information used in classifying associations in this respect was mainly obtained from a previous study of voluntary associations in the Sheffield/Rotherham area (Fosh, P., 'The embourgeoisement thesis: a critique and an alternative', unpublished undergraduate dissertation, University of Sheffield 1968) or where necessary by enquiring into specific cases.

Source: Adapted from Goldthorpe *et al.* (1968A), p.198.

NOTES

Notes to Introduction

1 Van de Vall (1970, p. 104) gives a very useful international comparison of branch meeting attendance figures.

2 For the problem of apathy in voluntary associations in general, see Barber (1950).

3 Sociologists in Britain who have been interested in grass-roots activism have looked instead at activism in political party constituencies.

4 Van de Vall (1970) summarises most of the sparse literature available.

5 Spinrad's article leaves much to be desired. He treats his material very uncritically and mixes together good statistical material with unsubstantiated generalised assertions, individual case histories, casual remarks – treating them all as giving equal support to his conclusions. However, Spinrad's article has been widely referred to as the definitive account of local actives' characteristics in the USA and has also been considered by some British sociologists to be applicable, to at least a significant extent, to branch activism in Great Britain.

Notes to Chapter 1

1 Only Wilensky (1956), in fact, uses such measures.

2 The tone of the advertisements placed in newspapers such as *The Guardian* by Aims of Industry during the miners' strike in 1974 were especially virulent.

3 Goldstein had an 'active core' of only 19 TGWU branch members. Moreover, Goldstein's work has been strongly criticised for being based on one rather atypical branch of the TGWU which had an extremely low level of participation by any standards. See Clegg (1952).

4 Both Newton (1969) in his study of the British Communist Party and Taylor (1974) in his short article on Communism in the British trade union movement emphasise that the Communist Party in Britain makes a point of encouraging its members to take part in trade union affairs.

5 It is also interesting to note here that Popitz *et al.* (1969, pp. 308–9, 313–7), writing on steelworkers in Western Germany, and Van de Vall (1970 pp. 149–50), in his study of a Dutch trade union and a Dutch political party, maintained that the Marxist trade union members they encountered were alienated both from politics and trade unionism and took part in neither.

6 We can also note here that Van de Vall (1970, pp. 161–4) proposed a theory of trade union participation that resembled the 'stake-in-the-job' theorists' proposition for job satisfaction. However, Van de Vall took a wider view of satisfaction and included, as well as job satisfaction,

satisfaction with the work community and with society. (It should also be commented upon that Van de Vall's statistical treatment of his work is rather elementary and his data do not always substantiate his arguments.)

7   However, both Tannenbaum and Kahn, and Dean proposed that there were exceptions to the relationship between activity and satisfaction with management: that under conditions of continued aggressive conflict, hostility might differentiate the actives from the inactives. However, Tannenbaum (1965, p. 747) strongly maintains that research in general supports the activity/management satisfaction relationship.

8   This is following Tannenbaum and Kahn's argument. Dean postulated that participation came about through the feeling of personal identification and responsibility. Tannenbaum and Kahn, however, suggest that in addition the union is an instrumentality for the worker's end of protecting his job interest. Thus the worker is active 'not exclusively through identification but largely through 'self-interest' (1958, p. 105).

9   Tannenbaum and Kahn (1958, pp. 138–9) found that actives took up their grievances more aggressively than inactives. They interpret this finding in the light of their other findings on perception of the company, not as indicating that the actives are hostile to the company, but as demonstrating the actives' desire to protect their 'job interests'.

10 The work produced by Form and Dansereau, in their study of a United Automobile Workers' local in Michigan, clearly shows in empirical terms the link between activity and job satisfaction: thus those members who attended union meetings or voted in union elections, more frequently liked their jobs than those who did not undertake these activities. Dean's data show a significant relationship between satisfaction with work tasks performed and meeting attendance in one of her locals, but not in a second. However, Dean's data do show that in both of these two locals, meeting attendance was significantly related to seeing more of work friends outside of work. (Questions on work tasks and leisure associates were not asked in her third local.) Satisfactory evidence is also produced by Tannenbaum and Kahn for their very similar contention that the actives show job satisfaction by having more friends at work than inactive members. Seidman et al., however, confine themselves merely to commenting that local leaders experienced greater job satisfaction than the rank-and-file. Moreover, there is little evidence to disprove this relationship: only Sayles and Strauss (1967, p. 59) claim – unsubstantiated by any quantitative material – that, in their study of 20 local units in the garment industry in New York state, local leaders considered their job unsatisfactory.

11 Dean, Rose (who studied a Teamsters' local in the Midwest), Purcell and Kerr all provide empirical material that amply demonstrates the relationship between favourable feelings towards the union and favourable feelings towards the management or company. However, Willerman's study must be noted here as an exception; he found a small but significant negative correlation between union and management identification (Willerman, B., 'Group identification in industry', Doctoral Dissertation, University of Michigan, 1949, p. 101). Dean empirically demonstrates her case that this dual allegiance is significantly related to meeting attendance where there are harmonious company-union relations but not where there are hostile relations. However, we must note that she changes the items used to measure attitude towards management between the surveys of her two locals with the more harmonious company-union relations and the survey of her local with hostile relations. The items used in her third local were a great deal more provocative than those used in her first two.

Purcell, in his discussion of the relationship between dual allegiance and participation, states that 88% of his stewards had dual allegiance compared to 74% of male members and 71% of female members. However, since he gives no indication whatsoever of his sample sizes, it is difficult to evaluate his findings.

12 Dean produces empirical data, as part of her study of dual allegiance, showing that where harmonious management-union relations exist, those who attend meetings are *more* favourable towards management. Similarly, Tannenbaum and Kahn provide data proving their slightly different argument that their actives in their three locals with harmonious company-union relations were not distinguished from the inactives by their *greater* hostility towards the company nor by any *greater* tendency to perceive a cleavage between company and union. Again, Purcell shows that there were no differences between stewards and other members in terms of their 'company allegiance'. In the case of the proposed exception of locals with hostile company-union relations, Tannenbaum and Kahn's data support their argument that hostility towards the company differentiates actives and inactives, but an analysis of Dean's data does not, in fact, show anti-management workers in her local with hostile relations to be significantly more likely to attend meetings than pro-management workers.

13 Tannenbaum and Kahn provide firm empirical support for the pay and skill contentions of this hypothesis, with the exception of their not finding a relationship between skill and activity in their local with conflicting company-union relations. Sayles and Strauss similarly provide firm empirical support here. Kyllonen, in his study of power and communication workers in Missouri, claims to have found a relationship between activity and pay, productivity and quality of work; however, his data do not, on statistical analysis, support his case. Seidman *et al.* and Purcell claim, but without substantiation, that their actives are drawn from the ranks of the highly skilled. On the other hand both Wilensky (1956, p. 118) in his study of Chicago car workers and Kornhauser *et al.* (1956, p. 153) in their study of Detroit car workers show empirically that socioeconomic status in their studies was not related to union activity or attachment. Furthermore, Form and Dansereau (1957, p. 11) found that their least active groups contained the greatest proportion of skilled workers. In addition, there is no evidence that the active members are any more highly educated than the inactive members in the USA (Tannenbaum and Kahn 1958, pp. 116–7; Kornhauser *et al.* 1956, p. 153; Rose 1952, p. 175). Form and Dansereau (1957, p. 11) found inactive members to be more highly educated than active.

14 Dean's data show a significant relationship between seniority and meeting attendance in all three of her locals. Tannenbaum and Kahn found that job seniority was related to activity in some locals but not in others. Seidman *et al.* and Sayles and Strauss comment on the importance of seniority in the explanation of activity, but provide no material to substantiate their claim. On the other hand, Lipset and Gordon's (1953, pp. 498–9) data show the active members to have had much greater job mobility than the inactive members.

15 Tannenbaum and Kahn demonstrate a significant relationship in their four locals between age and activity. Lipset *et al.* in their study of New York printers also provide material clearly showing older members to be more likely to be active in union politics than younger ones, but they interpret their finding as supporting their argument on the crucial role of the occupational community in stimulating political activity. On the other

hand, both Rose (1952, p. 168) and Kyllonen (1951, p. 531) demonstrate a curvilinear relationship between age and activity. Kornhauser *et al.* (1956, p. 153) and Dean (1954B, p. 53) found *no* relationship between age and activity and Seidman *et al.* (1958, p. 170) comment, although without substantiation, that local leaders were the same age on the whole as ordinary members. Finally here, Wilensky's study (1956, pp. 118–9) suggests that the activist is *younger* than the inactive member.

16 Both Kornhauser *et al.* and Rose provide empirical support for their claim that men are more likely to be active than women. Sayles and Strauss and Seidman *et al.* comment that women are generally not so active, but produce no data to substantiate this claim. On the other hand, Dean (1954B, p. 53) and Wilensky (1956, p. 118) found no significant relationship between sex and activity.

17 Tannenbaum and Kahn found a significant relationship between marital status and activity in two of their locals. In their other two locals they did not find a significant relationship, but they point out this might be due to the fact that almost all the members of these locals were married. Kyllonen (1951, p. 53) produces data which he claims show that single members are more likely to attend meetings than married members. However the correct statistical interpretation of his findings is that there is no difference between the married and unmarried in this respect.

18 Tannenbaum and Kahn (1958, pp. 117–122) are the only proponents of the 'stake-in-the-job' theory to investigate members' perception of the role of the union and these authors' findings do not by any means unconditionally support their contentions. While these authors found that their actives were generally more likely to endorse as union goals the improvement of wages and working conditions, the actives did not endorse fringe benefits to any greater extent than the inactives; furthermore these authors did *not* ask their active and inactive respondents whether they endorsed what, according to the 'stake-in-the-job' theory, should have been the most important union goal: the processing of job grievances.

19 For example, Seidman *et al.*'s question 'Do you like your work?' (1958, p. 287) and Dean's question 'How well do you like the actual job operations at (AMOCO, FANE)?' (1954B, p. 51).

20 This point has also more recently been made by Goldthorpe *et al.* (1968A, p. 11).

21 This point applies especially to Seidman *et al.*'s work. Although they followed up 'Do you like your work?' with the question 'Why do you say that?' they do not appear to analyse their workers' responses to this. Form and Dansereau's index of plant integration refers in a generalistic way to satisfaction with the job and department 'as a place to work'.

22 Morse in 1953 first took into account workers' levels of expectation in the assessment of their job satisfaction. This argument was later considerably developed by Goldthorpe *et al.* (1968A, pp. 36–42).

23 Beynon and Blackburn (1972, pp. 55–6) in Great Britain show that a worker can have a critical opinion of supervisory staff at the same time as having favourable opinions of 'top management'. Similarly, McCarthy and Parker (1968, p. 57) show that members' allegiance to the union is often primarily allegiance to the shop stewards and their own workshops and this allegiance, owing to multi-unionism, can effectively cross cut any allegiance to the national union.

24 Firm evidence that men are more likely to be shop stewards or otherwise active in the union is available from the government report, *Workplace Industrial Relations* (pp. 10, 115) – which supplies much useful information

on mainly manual shop stewards and rank-and-file members of the TGWU, the AEU, the NUGMW, the ETU, the NUR and the AUBTW – and from Beynon and Blackburn's (1972, p. 125) study of shop-floor workers in the food industry in Brompton.

25 Data from *Workplace Industrial Relations* (pp. 11, 115) show stewards to be significantly more likely to be skilled than ordinary members. There is also some evidence that active members are a little more highly educated than inactive ones, particularly with respect to further education *(Workplace Industrial Relations,* p. 135 and from Pedler's study of Sheffield steel workers 1973/74, p. 48).

26 Data from *Workplace Industrial Relations* (p. 134) show a significant relationship between length of service in firms and being a shop steward. Beynon and Blackburn (1972, p. 129) found stewards on day-shift had significantly longer service with their company than had rank-and-file members, but this relationship did not hold for night-shift workers.

27 Data from *Workplace Industrial Relations* (p. 133) clearly show a curvilinear relationship between age and being a shop steward. Beynon and Blackburn (1972, p. 129) found their stewards on the day-shift to be significantly older than rank-and-file members – however, this relationship broke down for the night-shift. Pedler (1973/4, p. 47) suggested that trade union representatives were younger on average than were the rank-and-file members.

28 One the one hand, Cousins (1972, pp. 226–7) shows that shop stewards and rank-and-file members among his Tyneside shopworkers thought it right to follow procedure in dispute and, in addition, that his stewards were more likely than the rank-and-file to consider productivity bargaining 'a good idea'. (His further claim that stewards were more willing than the rank-and-file to approve of local specific wage strikes is not substantiated by his data.) Similarly Dennis *et al.* (1956, pp. 97–116), in their descriptive account of the coal-mining industry, suggest that the rank-and-file are more in opposition to management than are branch officials. On the other hand, both Beynon (1973, pp. 197–9) in his study of Ford workers at Liverpool and Batstone *et al.* (1977, pp. 24–6, 266) in their study of vehicle builders, note that while both stewards and rank-and-file workers had conflicting views of industry and a 'working class factory consciousness', that of the stewards was more pronounced and closely tied up with their ideological beliefs. In addition to these opposing viewpoints, there are the findings of the report *Workplace Industrial Relations* (pp. 143, 145), those of Parker's 1972 (pp. 58, 66, 68–70) and 1973 (pp. 69, 73, 81, 83) reports (these being concerned with workers in the distributive trades, metal handling and other manufacturing industries, and public industries) and those of Pedler's (1973/74, p. 48) study, all of which indicate that no firm conclusions can be drawn on the question of the shop stewards' aggressiveness towards management *vis-a-vis* that of the rank-and-file.

29 The only material available on active and inactive members' nuclear families in the UK is that of Goldstein's (1952, pp. 159, 169, 252) study of one branch of the TGWU, which shows active members to have a larger number of children under school-leaving age and other dependants.

30 Evidence here suggests that actives have less favourable opinions in respect of their wages and facilities (Beynon 1973, pp. 91–3, *Workplace Industrial Relations* p. 136).

31 Olson (1965, pp. 66–97) has produced the most recent and coherent argument here although he produces no empirical findings of his own to

substantiate it. Thus he argues that it is irrational for the individual to sacrifice his time, money and energy in participating in collective action in order to pursue those trade union goals, chiefly economic, which he holds in common with the other trade union members. This participation is irrational since, given that the branch membership is large, the individual's contribution is unlikely to have any appreciable effects upon the outcome of such action and any collective benefits will by definition be equally available to him whether he has contributed to the cost of achieving them or not. The empirical occurrence of participation in trade unionism is explained as either pathological or as a means of obtaining individual, non-collective goals, either economic selective benefits (such as friendly benefits or grievance processing) or social selective benefits (such as prestige and friendship).

32 Seidman *et al.* (1950, pp. 233—4) also found that while none of the local leaders admitted that the desire to get pay for union services made them active, some of them described others as being primarily interested in getting on the union payroll.

33 Kyllonen produces a series of tables to prove his case but a careful analysis of these shows that the relationships of both marital status and kin-visiting with meeting attendance are not significant; furthermore the relationship between married members' activity and childlessness is only suggestive and does not, as Kyllonen himself admits, apply in the case of the family including very young children. Sayles and Strauss, and Seidman *et al.* confine themselves to purely descriptive accounts.

34 The only significant non-US study to discuss the seeking of extrinsic individual ends in trade union participation is Van de Vall's (1970, pp. 164—78) in the Netherlands. He talks at some length of the psychological needs that trade union participation can satisfy, but in a generalised and impressionistic manner.

35 Also Seidman *et al.* (1958, p. 258) point out that a number of 'good union men' were offered management positions after they had held union leadership posts.

36 There is some relevant information in the British material on trade unions here. Both Clegg *et al.* (1961, pp. 138—142, 167—171) in their study of trade union officers and Beynon (1973, p. 228) show that substantial proportions of their samples of branch secretaries and shop stewards would like to be full-time union officials, but they do not suggest that this was the reason why their respondents took part in union activities. There is also some empirical British material showing that foremen are frequently ex-union officials but, again, these authors do not suggest that their foremen respondents were previously active in the branch in order to obtain their promotion (Poole 1974A, p. 63, Warr, P.B., Bird, M., and Hadfield, R. W. 'Some characteristics of foremen in the iron and steel in-dustry', *Occupational Psychology*, October 1966, pp. 203—14).

37 It is interesting to note that Denver and Bochel (1973, pp. 58—9) in Great Britain found in contrast that a *lack* of religious upbringing was related to radical activism.

38 Further support for this contention is indirectly provided by a substantial number of studies of political activism both in the USA and the UK which suggests that political party actives are both sociable and gregarious and derive a great deal of social satisfaction from their participation. See the studies quoted in Milbrath (1972, pp. 74—75) and Bochel (1965, pp. 186—9, 191—3).

39 Tannenbaum and Kahn, and Dean, as we saw previously, clearly show activity and number of friends at work to be related. Dean, however,

interprets her finding as indicating social integration and not the possession of sociable traits; Tannenbaum and Kahn accept both interpretations. Tannenbaum and Kahn (pp. 84–5) also empirically demonstrate that actives choose their outplant friends from a wider array of social groups than inactives, which the authors interpret as a sign of the actives' greater tendency to take part in social affairs generally. There is no comparable information for the UK.

40 'Helping round the house' included family duties, minding children, painting and decorating, gardening, allotments, poultry-keeping, rabbit-keeping and boot-repairing. However, we should note that a number of authors in both the USA and the UK assert that the active neglects his family life (Chinoy 1953, p. 160; Purcell 1953A, p. 217; Sayles and Strauss 1967, p. 60; Seidman et al. 1958, p. 159; Gouldner 1947, pp. 390–1; Kyllonen 1951, p. 531; Beynon 1973, p. 203). However, these authors content themselves with individual examples or generalised descriptions and produce no substantive evidence to support their assertions. The exception here is Kyllonen, who produces data which he claims show that the more a union member visits with, or is visited by, relatives, the less likely he is to attend meetings. However, as stated earlier, his data do not satisfactorily prove his point.

41 The only theorists to have specifically discussed the very important question of the interpretation of union goals possessed by the 'socially-orientated' member are Form and Dansereau in the USA. These authors claim that the group which participated most in the union was that 'socially orientated' towards the union, which saw the union's main function as 'providing a social world' for its members. However, the table they produce in their article does not show 'socially orientated' members to participate to any significantly greater extent than 'politically orientated' or 'economically orientated' members. However, Tannenbaum and Kahn (1958, pp. 125–6) did specifically ask all of their respondents, along with questions on the achievement of various economic and political goals, whether they felt their local should provide more social and recreational facilities. In fact their findings here clearly showed that neither actives nor inactives felt their local should provide more social and recreational facilities. However, these authors do not sufficiently take this negative finding into account when assessing the explanatory value of their social activity motive. When the impressive amount of material available in the UK, in Western Europe in general and even in the USA (to be reviewed in Chapter 6) strongly suggesting that active trade unionists are not concerned merely with creating a social milieu, but instead with the achievement of economic, political and social goals, is taken into account, the suggestion that the active has a 'social' interpretation of trade union goals becomes unconvincing.

42 Tannenbaum and Kahn in the USA provide empirical material showing that actives in general belonged to a greater number of extra-union organisations than inactives and favoured to a greater extent those whose appeal was based on social action, such as sports teams, fraternal groups and veteran's associations. Sayles and Strauss' work also empirically supports this contention, although their evidence is much less substantial. On the other hand, Lipset and Gordon (1953, pp. 497–8) found no difference between active and inactive unionists in belonging to voluntary associations. While Kyllonen claims that those attending union meetings regularly attend meetings of other formal organisations regularly, his data do not statistically support his assertions, but suggest rather that there is no difference here between those who attend union meetings and those who do not. In the UK, Goldstein's material suggests that members of his

active sample were a little more likely than those of his inactive sample to belong to other working class organisations and, in addition, we can note that Bochel's (1965, pp. 38–40) study of ward secretaries in the Labour and Conservative Parties suggests that, while membership in voluntary associations may be of little importance in distinguishing the active from the inactive, office-holding may be of considerable importance. Finally Pedler (1973/4 p. 48) suggests, although he produces no data to substantiate his claim, that union representatives are more likely both to belong to more voluntary associations and to hold more offices in those they belong to than are members.

43   Although Kyllonen claims to have found that union meeting attenders are more likely than non-union meeting attenders to play cards, go fishing, go 'downtown' on Saturdays and attend church, the differences are much too small to support his claims. We can note, however, that the union itself can become an area of leisure-type functions for the active unionist (Purcell 1953A, pp. 205–6; Sayles and Strauss 1967, pp. 64, 69–70; Kovner and Lahne 1953, p. 11; Beynon 1973, p. 204).

44   Tannenbaum and Kahn (1958, pp. 149–55) propose that a syndrome of motives accounts for local activity and they include here, among others, the stake-in-one's-job and social activity. However, they give no indication of the relative importance of each of their themes.

45   See for example, Scott et al. (1956); Sayles, L.R., Behaviour of Industrial Work Groups (New York: Wiley, 1958); Woodward, J., Management and Technology (London: HMSO, 1958); and Goldthorpe, J. 'Technical organisation as a factor in supervisor-worker conflict' BJS, Vol. x, No. 3 (1959).

46   Neither Sayles and Strauss nor Seidman et al. produce any worthwhile empirical data to support their case. Tannenbaum and Kahn found that while on the one hand there was no relationship at all between job accessibility and union activity, on the other, there clearly was between activity and the two factors, department and shift location. It is also interesting to note here that Batstone et al.'s (1977, Chapter 6) study of shop stewards, which is an excellent piece of work in many respects, tends to adopt a socio-technical explanation for the predominance of leader-stewards in the assembly shop, stressing the frequent nature of crises associated with the highly integrated nature of the work in that shop and the larger size of the sections; this is accompanied by a distinct 'stopping short at the factory gate' in their approach to causality.

47   See for example D. Silverman's general critique 'Formal organisations or industrial sociology: towards a social action analysis of organisations', Sociology, Vol. 2, No. 2, May 1968, pp. 221–38; or that by Goldthorpe et al. (1968A, Ch.3).

48   Title of an ESC publicity booklet. ESC subsequently became BSC in 1967.

49   The relationship between BISAKTA and the ISTC is complex. Representatives from The British Steel Smelters, Mill, Iron and Tinplate Workers' Association, The Associated Iron and Steel Workers of Great Britain and The National Steel Workers' Association, Engineering and Labour League set up in 1917 two bodies: a new union called The British Iron, Steel and Kindred Trades Association – termed for the purpose of the scheme the Central Association and a body called the Iron and Steel Trades Confederation to which all the unions, including the Central Association, had to be affiliated. The governing authority of the Confederation was to be a central executive council consisting of representatives of each of the executive councils of the affiliated bodies

and was advised by a Central Committee composed of the general secretaries of these trade unions. The Central Association was to be exclusively the union to which workers organised after the scheme came into force were to be attached. At the same time, the other trade unions were to discontinue taking new members and it was also possible for members of these other trade unions to transfer to the Central Association. Two other steel unions eventually joined the Confederation – The Amalgamated Association of Steel and Iron Workers of Great Britain and The Tin and Sheet Millmen's Association – and in time became merged with the other three in the Central Association.

The duality of the organisation and the division of functions is as follows. BISAKTA – the Central Association of the scheme – provides the basis of government and administration through its registered rules. It has an executive – its 'supreme governing and administrative authority' – and a network of branches distributed throughout the country. The Confederation is the recognised authority for all trade agreements, all negotiations with employers and is the spokesman on the steel industry to the government. It is also the body affiliated to the TUC and to all other national/international groups (Pugh, A. *Men of Steel,* London: ISTC, 1951). The steel workers in the plant at Sheffield referred to themselves as BISAKTA members and I shall follow their terminology throughout this study. There was some disadvantage in choosing respondents who belonged to this union as it has a more conservative reputation than the average, but on balance the advantages of choosing these particular respondents, whose conditions of work fulfilled the required criteria, outweighted the disadvantage.

Notes to Chapter 2

1 Actually, the very first fieldwork step consisted of extensive exploratory interviews with the BISAKTA district secretary for the Sheffield area, the branch secretaries of the Melting Shop and Bloom and Billet Mill branches and the managers of the two shops.

2 However, Tannenbaum and Kahn (1958, pp. 49, 57—70), while deliberately restricting their index of participation in the local to the measurement of formal participation, were at some pains to demonstrate empirically that those members formally active were also 'at the center of shop discussions of the union and union affairs' (p. 49). Similarly, Lipset *et al.* (1956, pp. 72—7), as well as devising an index of political activity in the union focused on formal participation, also looked at the relationship between members' various characteristics and such informal activities as talking about union politics and reading the union journal.

3 Details of the conduct of the participation survey and the questions included are given in Appendix 1.

4 In both cases these pubs were situated at some distance from the steelworks.

5 The appropriate date of the last branch meeting for each branch was included in the question wording.

6 The appropriate dates of the last election for each branch were included.

7 This list included all of the trade union educational courses offered in the Sheffield/Rotherham area for which information could be obtained.

8 The branch positions were all voluntary; there are no full time branch officials or shop stewards in BISAKTA.

9 The lists, both of union committees and of union positions, included as many as information could be obtained about and also included the

various joint consultation committees and positions, since the pilot study had shown the respondents to be confused as to which were which. The respondents' membership and holding of these latter committee and official positions were disregarded in the analysis.

10   See footnote 13 below and Appendix 1.

11   In comparing the two branches in terms of their levels of participation, the pertinent figures are the absolute numbers, not the percentages. This is because the numbers active in a branch tend to be constant whatever the size of the branch. Thus small branches tend to have a proportionally higher level of participation than large branches. Political and Economic Planning (1948, pp. 25–9).

12   There have been no studies in the UK of the amount of informal and shop participation undertaken by *all* of the workers belonging to a branch with which to compare the findings for this survey.

13   Certain categories of respondents were excluded from this final analysis of the participation questionnaire findings, on the grounds that their inclusion in either the active or inactive interview groups would introduce extraneous elements into the analysis and confuse the issue. Those excluded were (1) the very young respondents – those born during or after 1950; (2) the newcomers – those who had joined the steelworks less than one year before the participation questionnaire was conducted; (3) coloured Commonwealth immigrants and aliens in general, excluding those born in Eire or in Anglo-Saxon Commonwealth countries. In all, 26 respondents were excluded here, some on more than one count. Also excluded were 24 Bloom and Billet Mill members made redundant between the participation survey and the main interview survey.

14   One respondent originally classified as active by the scoring system was subsequently declassified, since his total score unduly reflected the number of grievances he had asked the branch to take up on his behalf during the previous year; see Appendix 1.

Notes to Chapter 3

1   See Appendix 2 for details of the conduct of the survey and questions asked in the interview. See Appendix 4 for details of the statistical techniques – and abbreviations – employed.

2   The age breakdown by activity was 24 younger and 42 older actives, 31 younger and 28 older inactives. Where there are important differences between the age groups these are referred to in the text, otherwise only the findings for the total group are commented upon.

3   See the example given in the interview schedule in Appendix 2.

4   The degree of association (G) between rating a strong and active union branch highly and activity was moderate at 0.37. This finding can very easily be explained as an expression of the actives' greater belief in trade unionism, more evidence of which we shall encounter later.

5   It should be noted, however, that when the respondents were asked how the foreman should have to behave for the respondent to get along well with him, the actives were a little more likely to stress 'by not interfering' whereas the inactives were a little more likely to stress 'by showing interest'.

6   By asking the respondent a number of questions on his satisfaction with various aspects of his job rather than one general question, it was also hoped to avoid putting the worker on the defensive: with questions on ten different aspects of his work situation, it was thought highly probable that every worker could state his satisfaction with at least one aspect and

thus retain his self-esteem *vis-a-vis* the interviewer.

7 See the example given in the interview schedule in Appendix 2. However, the steelworkers' satisfaction with two job aspects – those of interest taken by management in the respondent as a person and opportunity to talk to other people when working – were measured differently (see Questions 10 and 12 in the interview schedule). This different form of question in the case of management's personal interest in the worker was adopted on the grounds that some steelworkers might resent rather than appreciate this and in the case of talking opportunity, to save interview time by utilising the interview question on job accessibility (see below).

8 In the case of satisfaction with pay, see below for the steelworkers' opinions on whether BSC could afford to pay higher wages.

9 We should also note here that the active and inactive respondents' reasons for getting along well with their foreman also differed: the actives were again a little more likely to stress the 'not interfere' aspect. However, in contrast to our previous finding regarding the respondents' expectation of this job aspect, the inactives were not any more likely than the actives to stress the 'show interest' aspect.

10 I. e. people tend to rate something they are heavily committed to as more satisfactory than do those who are not so involved.

11 Tannenbaum and Kahn contended that the active has more 'friends' at work than the inactive member.

12 Dean contended that those who attend branch meetings see more of their workmates outside of work than those who do not attend.

13 The remaining 8 actives and 6 inactives chose the proferred 'don't know' category.

14 The third most frequently given reason was that management took an interest in the workers, given by 6 actives (13%) and 7 inactives (17%).

15 Three actives and 6 inactives were 'not sure' if they wanted to become a shift foreman or not and only 11 actives and 5 inactives felt they would like to become a shift foreman 'very much indeed' or 'quite a lot'.

16 The active and inactive groups did differ however, in the nature of their second and third most frequently given reasons for not wanting to become a shift foreman (respondents could give more than one reason). Thus for the actives, the second most frequently given reason referred to ideological objections (given by 13 (25%) actives) and the third referred to a possible drop in wages (given by 12 (23%) actives). For the inactives the second most frequently given reason was lack of ability or education (given by 12 (25%) inactives) followed by ideological objections (given by 9 (19%) inactives).

17 Four actives and 4 inactives answered 'mildly approve' or 'strongly approve' and 3 inactives and 2 actives chose the proferred 'don't know' reply.

18 Forty-two out of 44 actives (95%) gave this reply as did all 33 of the inactives.

19 All of the 16 actives here gave this reply together with 18 out of the 19 inactives (95%).

20 The active respondents, in particular the older actives, were, in fact, much more likely to have had a grievance at work than the inactives: 49 out of 66 actives (74%) compared to 25 out of 59 inactives (42%). This finding will be returned to in Chapter 5 where the differing experiences of adversity of actives and inactives are discussed.

21 It should be noted, however, that the number of grievances personally placed by a branch member during the year preceding the interview was

one of the factors utilised to determine an individual's participation score. See Appendix 1.

22 Tannenbaum and Kahn (1958, pp. 138—9) also found that their actives were very much more aggressive with regard to taking up grievances, while closely resembling the inactives in their perception of their company and in their feeling about a union officer becoming a foreman. These authors, however, conclude that their actives were motivated here by the desire to protect their job interests. This explanation has not been adopted here since, as we shall see in the concluding chapter, there was little support in the survey findings for the 'stake-in-the-job' theory in general, while, on the other hand, significant support was found for the view that the active members had a considerably different orientation from the inactive ones towards trade unionism.

23 In the case of the respondents' comparison of BSC's management, the replies 'very much better' and 'quite a bit better' than most other firms were grouped together as were the other four replies of 'about average', 'quite a lot worse', 'very much worse' and 'don't know'. In the case of the respondents' satisfaction with their branch's performance, ratings of 75 and over were grouped together as were ratings of 74 and below.

24 For the construction of this new variable, which shall be called 'work task satisfaction', the respondents' ratings were grouped into two categories, those with ratings of 75 and over and those with ratings of 74 and under. In the case of number of workmates seen outside of work, the respondents were grouped into those with one or more and those with none and, in the case of seniority rating, the respondents were grouped into those who had been employed at the steelworks for seven years or less and those who had been employed there for eight years (i.e. from when the plant was opened).

25 Four out of 59 inactives (7%) also had a score of 3 on the 'social integration' variable.

26 As was the case with dependent children, the degree of association between activity and total number of children increased for those respondents under 40 to 49. Activity and total number of children were not significantly related for those aged 40 or more.

27 Kin members were defined to include parents, siblings and their families, together with respondents' own wives and children and their children's families if applicable.

28 Information on respondents' membership of political parties was collected as part of the question on respondents' membership/participation in non-union voluntary associations, see Appendix 2.

29 The voluntary associations named by the respondents were classified in terms of the specificity of their function and the probable social composition of their membership (see Appendix 4). However, the survey revealed no differences between the active and inactive respondents in the *type* of voluntary association to which they belonged. By far the most popular individual categories were those of diffuse function organisations with predominantly manual worker members – respondents referred here mainly to working men's clubs – and that of intermediate function organisations with occupational mixed membership – respondents referred here mainly to BSC clubs; 57 out of 61 actives (93%) and 41 out of 53 inactives (77%) belonged to one or more of the former type and 44 actives (72%) and 34 inactives (64%) belonged to one or more of the latter.

30 Again, there was no difference between the active and inactive groups in the type of voluntary associations in which they took an active part, in

terms of either the nature of their functions or the probable composition of their membership. By far the most popular individual category was that of diffuse function organisations composed predominantly of manual workers – respondents here mainly referred as previously to working mens' clubs; 53 out of 61 actives (87%) and 35 out of 53 inactives (66%) belonged to one or more voluntary associations in this category.

31 The shifts on which the respondent worked during the week preceding the interview obviously greatly influenced the amount of social activity he was able to undertake. In the survey it was not possible to control directly for this due to the steelwork's system of rotation; it was possible however, to total the number of mornings, afternoons, nights, days off, days (in the case of day men) worked by the active and inactive respondents. It was found here that in all categories the actives' and inactives' totals were very similar.

32 The degree of association was only modest, however, at 0.29.

33 The respondent's scores for these two categories of social activity were included in the calculation of their total number of social activities taken part in during the week preceding the interview.

34 There were no significant differences in the relationships between the social activity measures and branch activity between younger and older members.

35 In both the Melting Shop and the Bloom and Billet Mill the work was organised on a system of rotating shifts, so that a worker was not permanently on mornings, afternoons or nights. Some sections within each shop had a 3-shift rotating system whereas others had a 4-shift one; this meant that the different groups of workers changed over shifts at different times. These factors may have inhibited the development of 'mutual interests'.

36 In fact, the relationship between working in the Furnace or Casting Bay and activity was significant at the 0.05 level using the X^2 test and the degree of association (θ) was 0.29.

37 The mean job percentage bonus ratings for the Bloom and Billet Mill departments were for the Heating Section 61.8%, for the Rolling Section 64.8% and for the Finishing End 60.0%.

Notes to Chapter 4

1 The younger actives were slightly, though not significantly or suggestively so in statistical terms, more likely to give instrumental-individual reasons for joining: thus 9 out of 24 younger actives (38 per cent) referred to this type of motivation compared to 11 out of 42 older actives (26 per cent).

2 It would have been better in fact to have included a second question in the interview here such as: If yes, ask: 'Have you ever done anything about it?'.

3 There were no differences by age, however, in the case of active and inactive respondents' views of trade unions' political and social roles.

4 The members advocated such aims here as 'they should find different ways of negotiating with management without having them strikes all the time' and 'they should get management and workers all working together'.

5 Fifteen actives and 15 inactives felt that trade unions should only be concerned with pay and conditions and a further 5 actives and 6 inactives gave 'don't know' replies to this question.

6 There was in fact a significant difference between the active and inactive groups in their tendency to give 'don't know' replies, when asked what

trade unions should try and achieve in political life: 44 per cent of the inactives (20 out of 45) compared to 11 per cent of the actives (6 out of 53) gave such a reply. The level of significance here, using a X^2 test, was significant at the 0.001 level and the degree of association (θ) between giving a 'don't know' reply and inactivity was 0.42.

7 One inactive gave a 'don't know' reply to this question and one active and one inactive preferred not to answer.

8 An example regarding the improvement of the quality of working life is the comment of one respondent that 'They (the trade unions) should make sure an ordinary working man has a good life, not just going to work and going to bed'.

9 The respondents' views on the role of trade unions in future change were investigated during the unstructured discussion on class and society which came at the end of the interview. See Appendix 5.

10 The emphasis by about a third of the actives in total on the role of specific incidents/particular situations will be echoed, as we shall see later in Chapter 5, by the survey's findings on the active and inactive steelworkers' general experience of strikes.

11 Cousins and Brown (1972). Details of the methods used in the survey to obtain data on the steelworkers' images of society are given in Appendix 5, together with a discussion on the findings for the sample as a whole.

12 It is interesting to note here that only 3 actives referred to the also ideologically-orientated class criterion of 'power'.

13 The absolute proportions were: 34 out of 62 actives believed a conflict of interests existed, while 28 did not; 27 out of 54 inactives did, while 27 did not.

14 It was decided not to use the kind of statement choice question often used in surveys of workers' attitudes (e.g. Goldthorpe *et al.* 1968A, Wedderburn, D., 'What determines shopfloor behaviour?', *New Society*, vol. 21, no. 512, pp. 128–130), because it was found that the two alternative 'football' statements as they are usually worded did not appear clearly contradictory to respondents in the pilot survey, who found it possible to agree with elements of both statements. Thus, forcing the respondent to choose one or other of the statements would not, it was felt, yield meaningful results. Consequently in the main interview survey the steelworkers were asked how much they agreed or disagreed with two separate statements, one suggesting a harmonious relationship and the other a conflicting one.

15 The survey results showing how far the steelworkers agreed and disagreed with the two statements on worker-management relations in society certainly demonstrates the methodological problems involved in using the 'football' statement choice measure. Indeed 23 respondents overall felt able to agree or disagree with both statements.

16 The absolute figures were, for those satisfied, 27 out of 66 actives and 21 out of 59 inactives and, for those dissatisfied, 36 actives and 35 inactives. Three actives and three inactives had no opinion here.

17 The absolute figures were 24 out of 36 actives and 17 out of 35 inactives opting for redistribution and 12 actives and 17 inactives opting for reconstruction. One inactive was dissatisfied with the present social structure but had no idea what changes he would like to see.

18 The absolute figures for voting Labour on the grounds that it represented the interests of the working class were 43 out of 54 actives and 27 out of 39 inactives. The next two most popular reasons for consistently voting Labour were: that the respondents approved of the Labour Party's

performance while in office (given by 7 (13 per cent) of the actives and 5 (13 per cent) of the inactives); and that the respondents' family and neighbourhood all voted Labour and/or they had been 'brought up' to vote Labour (given by 4 (7 per cent) of the actives and 9 (23 per cent) of the inactives).

19 No inactives belonged to a political party.

Notes to Chapter 5

1 The issue of causality did not play a prominent part in the 'stake-in-the-job' theory, as laid out by its major proponents. Activity was seen here as springing directly from specific factors such as skill level, seniority, age, marital status and size of family, which accounted for the actives' higher stake in the job and which, in turn, led to their greater participation in the union local.

2 See Seidman *et al.*'s (1958, p. 245) very generalised comments on the circumstances that produced their 'good union man'. Chinoy (1953, p. 166) talks about causal factors such as a 'dash of foreign radical flavouring'.

3 For the occupational classification used in this survey, see Appendix 7.

4 The one management workfriend named was excluded from the analysis of workfriends' characteristics.

5 For example see Dennis *et al.*'s (1956) study of coalminers and *The Dockworker* (1954).

6 Cannon has a similar argument for the pro-labour ideological ethos of British printers (1967, pp. 175–8).

7 The steelworkers in the sample did not in general, however, live in excessively working-class areas. Out of their four nearest neighbours, 17 out of 66 actives and 10 out of 58 inactives (one inactive lived in an isolated spot without neighbours) had at least one neighbour with an intermediate occupation and 29 actives and 18 inactives had at least one neighbour with a non-manual occupation.

8 Information was also collected on how convenient it was for the steelworkers to travel from their present homes to attend the branch meetings, held on Sunday mornings in pubs situated some distance from the steelworks and from the Sheffield and Rotherham city centres. Ease of getting to branch meetings was considered here since it was felt that such factors as bus routes, car ownership and traffic conditions rendered comparison of distance from respondents' homes to the branch meeting place in terms of mileage fairly meaningless. The results showed that there was no difference between the actives and inactives; the majority of both groups – 48 out of 66 actives and 35 out of 59 inactives, when asked how easy it was for them to get to branch meetings in terms of travel, chose the replies 'very easy' or 'fairly easy'.

9 If respondents still lived with their parents, they were asked for details of their parents' tenure.

10 Thirty-three out of 64 respondents who rented their homes from the council lived in semi-detacheds, 5 lived in maisonettes, 5 lived in flats, 4 lived in detached houses and 17 lived in terraced houses. Out of 64 respondents who rented from the council, 61 had homes that were built between 1930 and 1969; only 7 respondents had homes built before 1930.

11 Twenty-three out of 46 respondents who were owner-occupiers had bought houses in 'owner-occupied not select' enumeration districts, 7 in council housing dominated ones, 7 in rented accommodation dominated

ones, 6 in mixed tenure areas and only 3 in owner-occupied select areas.

12 Thirty-one of 46 owner-occupiers had bought semi-detached houses, 9 terraced houses and 6 detached houses. Thirty-one out of 46 owner-occupiers had bought homes built between 1930 and 1969, 8 had bought ones built prior to 1930 but not before 1890, and 3 ones built in 1970 or later. Four owner-occupiers did not know when their homes had been built.

13 Eight out of the 15 respondents who privately rented their homes lived in terraced houses, 5 in detached houses and 2 in flats. Twelve out of the 15 respondents here rented houses built between 1890 and 1920, 2 lived in ones built in the 1930s or 1940s, and one in one built during the 1840s.

14 One younger active steelworker was immensely impressed by the screening on television of Zola's novel *Germinal* and this he said was an important factor involved in his developing an interest in trade unionism.

Notes to Chapter 6

1 We should note here that Tannenbaum and Kahn do not systematically relate their findings on their active and inactive members' views on trade unions to their 'stake-in-the-job' contentions. Instead they believe that a 'syndrome of motives' accounts for trade union activity, the 'character' of the trade union playing an important part in determining which social and psychological factors move a member in a particular local to activity. However, the 'stake-in-the-job' motive is given most emphasis in their work (1958, p. 149). Seidman *et al.* (1951—2, p. 699) also provide some empirical support for the view that actives had a broader conception of trade union goals but their evidence is not detailed enough to permit an adequate assessment of its reliability. Miller and Young's (1955, p. 41) comments support this argument but are again insubstantive. See also here Seidman *et al.*'s (1958, pp. 244—6) descriptive account of their 'good union man', Sayles and Strauss (1967, p. 59) on their 'local-wide leader' and Gouldner (1947, pp. 389—90) on his 'progressive leader'. Seidman and his Chicago colleagues in their work (1950, pp. 230—3 and 1958, p. 1972) also give examples of the role of disagreeable individual or group experiences in members' becoming active in a local, and of the way in which leaders could 'accidentally' become active through pressure from their fellow members on a specific occasion and then carry on to become active on a permanent basis.

2 Beynon's study also emphasised the 'triggering off' effect of incidents 'on the line' in an active's development.

3 Batstone *et al.* also looked at the attitudes and behaviour of staff shop stewards – APEX and ACTSS – in the same firm, where there were considerable differences in trade union perception.

4 Reiner also refers to the importance in motivation of injustices either experienced or observed in the job.

5 While Tannenbaum and Kahn, and Rose, offered their respondents a selection of economic, political and social goals of trade union pursuit for their respondents to agree/disagree with, none of the goals as posed in their questionnaire can be described as radical. It is therefore open to speculation whether or not these authors' active members would have also agreed with the pursuit of trade union goals aimed at altering the present fabric of society.

6 See Miller and Young (1955, p. 41) and Seidman *et al.*'s (1958, pp. 242—6) description of their 'good union man'.

7   Seidman *et al.*'s (1958, pp. 242—6) description of their 'good union man'
    also suggests that he did not see employers in general as class enemies.

8   Denver and Bochel in fact found that the Communist Party activists were
    more likely to be trade union activists than were the Labour Party
    activists, although the difference here was not statistically significant.

9   While the older actives were more likely to be currently married than
    their inactive counterparts, this was mainly due to a greater number of
    the older inactives being separated, divorced or widowed. Indeed, older
    actives tended to have the same number of dependent children as their
    inactive counterparts.

10 Cousins (1972, pp. 226—7) does mention personal experience of striking,
    but in a confused manner. His table actually shows in statistical terms
    that stewards were significantly more likely than ordinary shipworkers
    to have experience of national strikes, but significantly less likely to have
    experience of local strikes on specific wage issues.

11 Bochel also includes here witnessing the plight of others as a factor.

12 See also Purcell's (1953A, p. 210) unsubstantiated comments on the
    importance of a pro-union family.

13 Unfortunately Beynon does not give a comparable figure for his rank-and-
    file car workers.

14 Denver and Bochel suggest that the influence of family of origin is much
    more important than that of a spouse – whose influence is more a
    reinforcing than a 'predisposing' or 'push' factor.

15 For the relationship between skilled status and social and political skills,
    see Newton (1969, pp. 62—4). For the relationship between low skill,
    deference and acceptance, see McKenzie, R.T. and Silver, A., *Angels in
    Marble* (London: Heinemann, 1968); Nordlinger, E. *The Working Class
    Tories* (London: MacGibbon and Kee, 1967) and Parkin (1971).

Notes to Chapter 7

1   Thus Scott *et al.* (1956, p. 112) state: 'In short, industrial relations in the
    (steel) industry have been characterized from the early years by an
    endeavour to resolve disputes by negotiation, conciliation and arbitration
    rather than by recourse to more drastic measures, and by a recognition
    on the part of management and the unions of each others' difficulties and
    needs'. However, also see Pedler's (1973/4, pp. 58—9) views on the
    specificity of findings of studies of the steel industry, especially his doubts
    of there being a unique union-management climate in steel, for either
    the UK or other countries.

2   Seidman *et al.*'s (1958, Chapter 2) description of a miners' community
    in the USA shows many similarities.

3   Bott, E., *Family and Social Network* (London: Tavistock, 1957) and
    Hoggart, R., *The Uses of Literacy* (London: Pelican, 1958). However, in
    a later article Lockwood (1975, pp. 239—42) points out that his 1966
    article was concerned only to show how communal sociability and
    dichotomous imagery were sustained by certain forms of work and
    community relations, and not to provide an account of working-class
    consciousness. Thus he argues that work and community relations
    provide only the most elementary matrix of sentiments out of which a
    variety of political class consciousnesses may be fashioned.

4   Popitz *et al.*, however, qualify this by saying that these demands for
    radical reform may represent a heritage from Marxism, which has been
    introduced into the available repertoire of contemporary criticism, but

which now has little to do with real hopes and wishes (1969, p. 312). But the point remains that at some time, according to Popitz et al., this belief was held by a substantial body of workers.

5　For a description of 'business unionism' in the USA, where trade unions are said to pursue their own narrow self-interests, to be wholly concerned with pay increases, and to be decentralised and locally orientated, see Lipset, S.M. 'The labour movement and American values' in Laslett, J. H. and Lipset, S.M. (eds.) *Failure of a Dream? Essays in the History of American Socialism* (New York: Anchor Press/Doubleday, 1974). However, there appear to be few specific surveys demonstrating that blue-collar workers in the USA hold this particular view of trade unionism, apart from MacKenzie's (1973) study of craft workers in Providence. In addition, several recent political studies have indicated that the Democratic Party is more closely linked with the US trade unions than is commonly supposed (see, for example, Greenstone, D., *Labour in American Politics,* Chicago: University of Chicago Press, 1977). This leads one to question just how widespread this type of unionism is among US blue-collar workers.

6　However, it should be noted that, in Goldthorpe *et al.*'s study, the craftsmen took a significantly greater interest in branch unionism and were more likely to profess an intrinsic belief in trade unionism. The craftsmen were, in fact, in a number of respects a deviant group, being less instrumentally orientated to work.

7　Goldthorpe *et al.,* however, saw the situation in the late 1960's as an 'open' one, and considered that the Labour Party had the opportunity for creative political leadership by mobilising workers' hitherto sub-political grievances, demands, and aspirations into a sociopolitical force (pp. 188–195).

8　Beynon (1973, p. 13) describes the Labour Party as now 'atrophied' and 'stripped of all but the most brazen pretentions to radicalism'.

9　However, Goldthorpe *et al.*'s study was not designed to distinguish between active and inactive trade union members. It is possible, had these authors looked specifically at their active members, that these affluent workers might have been found to differ in the extent to which they were committed intrinsically to trade unionism: the definition of 'active' would of course have to cover both branch *and* shop participation. Beynon's description of his rank-and-file members as tending to view their trade union as a service organisation fits in with this argument. However, in the Luton study, had the most active members in overall terms (who would *not* of necessity have been the craftsmen) possessed a strong intrinsic commitment to trade unionism lacking in their fellow members, it seems unlikely that it would not have been commented on by the authors.

10　Goldthorpe (1967) identifies solidaristic and instrumental collective action with Weber's *Wertrational* and *Zweckrational* action. Popitz *et al.* (1969, p. 312) in West Germany put forward a similar argument that their second type of dichotomous consciousness (where society was seen as a 'progressive ordered structure' was taking the place in trade unionism of their fifth dichotomous type (where society was seen as a 'class society' in need of 'reform') due to the rise in affluence of the working class.

11　For early American radicalism see Laslett, J.H.M. 'Socialism and American trade unionism' and Dubojsky, M. 'Socialism and Syndicalism', both in Laslett, J.H.M. and Lipset, S.M. *op. cit.* In Guérin, D., *100 years of Labour in the USA* (London: Links, 1979) see particularly the account of the political mobilisation of the rank-and-file in the International Brotherhood of Teamsters, in the Introduction by Amsden, J.

12　Hartz. L. *The Liberal Tradition in America* (New York: Harcourt,

Brace and World, 1955). See also Sombert's arguments, Sombert, W., *Why is there no socialism in the USA?* (London: Macmillan, 1976).

13   See also, however, Lockwood's (1975, p. 250) defence of his earlier propositions concerning the traditional proletarian worker – although it should be noted that in his final paragraph Lockwood admits that the concept of the traditional worker may perhaps be considered to have 'after all succumbed to facts'. Marsden, R. and Duff, E. *Workless* (Harmondsworth: Pelican, 1975).

14   Westergaard and Resler (1975, pp. 408–21) document the 'crumbling of institutional compromise' and the 'drift to the left within the labour movement' in the 1960s and early 1970s.

15   The 'trade unions in decline' theory has most prominently been put forward by: Galbraith, J. K., *The New Industrial State* (Harmondsworth: Pelican, 1969); Lester, R.A., *As Unions Mature* (Princeton: Princeton University Press, 1958); Kerr, C., Dunlop, J.T., Harbison, F.M. and Myers, C.A., *Industrialism and Industrial Man* (London: Heinemann, 1962); Bell, D., *The End of Ideology* (New York: The Free Press, 1960) and Blauner (1964).

16   Blauner's (1964, pp. 11–13) empirical evidence in the case of the chemical industry consisted of a reworking of the rather dated Roper survey (conducted in 1947 for *Fortune* magazine), and his own very limited case study of the Bay Chemical Company (although this was supplemented by Davis' job-attitude survey of the same plant).

17   This company-level trade unionism differs from craft unionism in two fundamental ways: (1) the stress laid on economic phenomena; (2) the narrowness of the 'company spirit' which leads to a sharper isolation of the working-class sections employed in the advanced industrial sectors than was the case with craft corporatism. Mallet (1975), p. 74.

18   See Gallie's (1978, p. 28) criticisms.

19   Goldthorpe *et al.* (1969, pp. 185–6) also feel that their empirical study contributes to the debate on the effect of advanced technology on worker attitudes and behaviour. While none of their groups of workers experienced such advanced technology as Gallie's did, they did experience several contrasting work environments from small batch to process production, yet the groups had similar attitudes and behaviour patterns, and a shared orientation to work and trade unionism. In addition Goldthorpe *et al.* maintain that their process workers – who worked within the most integrated production unit – were if anything less concerned than other groups with the possibilities for participation in the plant or work affairs generally, including trade unionism beyond the shop floor level.

20   Gallie notes here that he is not proscribing future development in trade union attitudes in the automated sector, but maintains: (1) that these will depend on changing broader structural and cultural factors rather than technological factors; and (2) that the automated sector will not be particularly distinctive but will be part of a very much broader movement occurring within industry in the particular society. Low-Beer's work on the new working class in Italy also stresses the importance of political traditions over organisational factors in determining strike participation: Low-Beer, J. R. *Protest and Participation* (Cambridge: Cambridge University Press, 1978).

21   Nor, for that matter, did either the French or British patterns of trade unionism resemble Mallet's description of trade unionism in the first half of the twentieth century.

22   Mann (1973) also strongly states that Great Britain (and the USA) has a

different type of trade unionism from France (and Italy), although Mann interprets this difference in accordance with his view of radicalism as a transitional phenomenon and the 'backwardness' of French and Italian capitalism. However the important point here is that Mann assumes that the French and British trade union movements were once similar in that they possessed radical, moderate and extreme conservative elements. Gallie's work argues strongly against such an approach.

23 Unfortunately, Gallie's survey of his refinery workers did not include questions on their attitudes towards the role of trade unions in society; he relied instead for his material on the analysis of trade union documents and interviews with shop stewards and branch officials. This makes a valid comparison with the findings on the Sheffield steel workers difficult.

Notes to Appendix 1

1 The reasons most frequently given by the non-respondents for not filling in the questionnaire were that the respondent's participation was the affair of the branch or respondent only, given by 6 out of 23 (26%), and that the respondent could not be bothered, given by 5 out of 23 (22%).

2 One respondent came into the 'don't know' category. However, the non-respondents' pattern of participation was not totally unlike that of the respondents. The table below compares the non-respondents and respondents' levels of activity. The respondents have been divided into groups corresponding to those of the non-respondents on the basis of their total participation scores; thus scores of 13 and over correspond to an 'a' rating, scores of 11 and 12 to a 'b' rating, scores of 8, 9 and 10 to a 'c' rating, scores of 6 and 7 to a 'd' rating and scores of 5 and under to an 'e' rating. From this table we can see that although there is no group among the non-respondents corresponding to the respondents' 'a' group, the non-respondents were slightly more likely than the respondents to come into the middle groups 'b' 'c' and 'd'. Thus it *cannot* be argued that the non-respondents were the most inactive members of the branch – so inactive that they did not even fill in the questionnaire – and that, in consequence this study is invalid because the social characteristics of the most active are not compared with those of the most inactive.

Rating	Non-respondents		Respondents	
a	0	0%	67	31%
b	3 ⎫		19 ⎫	
c	4 ⎬ 50%		48 ⎬ 41%	
d	4 ⎭		21 ⎭	
e	11	50%	62	29%
Total	22	100%	214	100%

Notes to Appendix 2

1 There were originally 69 active respondents selected. However, one became chronically ill and did not return to the steelworks, and one was reclassified as a moderate scorer and not as an active (see Appendix 1). The one active who refused to be interviewed gave no reason as did three of the four inactives who refused. The fourth inactive refused on the grounds that he disliked answering questions. The respondents who

refused to be interviewed did not differ from those who agreed to the interview in terms of age, skill level, or seniority.

2   Scales identical to that reproduced in question 1 were printed on the interview schedules for questions 2 to 8 (1).

3   Scales identical to that reproduced in question 16 were printed on the interview schedule for questions 17 to 25 (1).

4   The boxes were headed: strongly agree, mildly agree, neither agree nor disagree, mildly disagree, strongly disagree.

Notes to Appendix 4

1   The correction for continuity was used for all 2 x 2 X^2 tests.

2   See Freeman, L.C., *Elementary Applied Statistics* (London: Wiley 1965) pp. 71—8; and Weiss, R. S. *Statistics in Social Research* (London: Wiley, 1968), pp. 190—6.

3   See Freeman, *op. cit.*, pp. 108—19.

4   *Op. cit.* pp. 79—87. Activity was considered to be an ordinal scale.

Notes to Appendix 5

1   Adapted from Goldthorpe *et al.* (1969, p. 200).

2   Cousins and Brown (1972, pp. 17—20).

3   Although Popitz *et al.*'s (1969) classification of images yielded more meaningful results, and was perhaps more suitable for this study, the authors provide very little information on how they actually classified their raw data.

4   Cousins and Brown (1972, pp. 20—22).

5   Platt, J., 'Variations in answers to different questions on perceptions of class'. *Sociological Review*, vol. 19, no. 3, 1971, p. 417.

BIBLIOGRAPHY

Allen, V. L. 1957. *Trade Union Leadership* (London: Longmans)

Banks, J.A. 1963. *Industrial Participation* (Liverpool: Liverpool University Press)
1974. *Trade Unionism* (London: Collier-Macmillan).

Batstone, E., Boraston, I and Frenkel, S. 1977. *Shop Stewards in Action* (Oxford: Blackwell)

Barber, B. 1950. 'Participation and mass apathy in associations' in Gouldner, A.W., *Studies in Leadership* (New York: Harper)

Bealey, F., Blondel, J. and McCann, W.P. 1965. *Constituency Politics* (London: Faber and Faber)

Beynon, H. 1973. *Working for Ford* (Harmondsworth: Penguin)

Beynon, H., and Blackburn, R.M. 1972. *Perceptions of Work* (Cambridge: Cambridge University Press)

Blauner, R. 1964. *Alienation and Freedom* (Chicago: University of Chicago Press)
1960. 'Work satisfaction and industrial trends in modern society' in Galenson, W. and Lipset, S.M. (eds.), *Labour and Trade Unionism* (New York: Wiley)

Bochel, J.M. 1965. 'Activists in the Conservative and Labour Parties: a study of ward secretaries in Manchester' (unpublished MA thesis, University of Manchester)

Brown, R. and Brannen, P. 1970. 'Social relations and social perspectives among shipbuilding workers – a preliminary statement' Parts One and Two, *Sociology*, vol. 4, pp. 71–84, 197–216

Brown, R.K. 1973. 'Sources of objectives in work and employment' in Child, J., *Man and Organization* (London: Allen and Unwin)

Brown, R.K., Brannen P., Cousins, J.M. and Sampie, M.L. 1972. 'The contours of solidarity: social stratification and industrial relations in shipbuilding', BJIR, vol. x, no. 1 pp. 12–41

Cannon, I.C. 1967. 'Ideology and occupational community: a study of compositors *Sociology*, vol 1, no. 2, May, pp. 165–185

Chinoy, E. 1953. 'Local union leadership' in Gouldner, A.W. (ed), *Studies in Leadership* (New York: Harper)

Clegg, H.A. 1952. 'Democracy in a general union' *Socialist Commentary*, pp. 199–202
Municipal Workers (Oxford: Blackwell)

Clegg, H.A. Killick, A.J. and Adams, R. 1961. *Trade Union Officers* (Oxford: Blackwell).

Cousins, J. 1972. 'The non-militant shop steward', *New Society*, 3 February, pp. 226–228
1954. *General union: A Study of the National Union of General and*
Cousins, J. and Brown, R.K. 1972. 'Patterns of paradox – shipbuilding workers'

images of society', Paper presented to the SSRC Conference on The
Occupational Community of the Traditional Worker, Durham.

Cyriax, G. and Oakeshott, R. 1960. *The Bargainers* (London: Faber and Faber)

Dean, L.R. 1954A. 'Union activity and dual loyalty', *Industrial and Labour
Relations,* 7, pp. 526–36

    1954B. 'Social integration, attitudes, and union activity', *Industrial and
Labour Relations Review,* 8 October, pp. 48–58

Dennis, N., Henriques F. and Slaughter C. 1956. *Coal is Our Life* (London: Eyre
and Spottiswoode).

Denver, D.T. and Bochel, J.M. 1973. 'The political socialization of activists in the
British Communist Party', *BJPS,* 3, Part 1, January, pp. 53–71

Donnison, D.V. and Plowman, D.E.G. 1954. 'The functions of local Labour
Parties', *Political Studies,* vol. 2., no. 2., pp. 154–167

Durand, C. 1971A. 'Ouvriers et techniciens en mai·1968' in Dubois, P.,
Dulong, R., Durand, C., Erbes-Sequin, S. and Videl, D., *Grèves
Revendicatives ou Grèves Politiques?* (Paris: Anthropos)

    1971B. *Conscience Ouvrière et l'Action Syndicale* (Paris)

Ferris, P. 1972. *The New Militants: Crisis in the Trade Unions* (Harmondsworth,
Penguin)

Form. W.M. and Dansereau, H.K. 1957. 'Union member orientations and patterns
of social integration', *Industrial and Labour Relations Review,* 11, October,
pp. 3–12

Galenson, W. 1961. *Trade Union Democracy in Western Europe* (Berkeley:
University of California Press)

Gallie, D. 1978. *In Search of the New Working Class* (Cambridge, CUP)

Giddens, A. 1973. *The Class Structure of the Advanced Societies* (London:
Hutchinson)

Goldstein, J. 1952. *The Government of British Trade Unions* (London: Allen and
Unwin)

Goldthorpe, J. 1967. Book review of Olson, M. *The Logic of Collective Action* in
Sociology, vol. 3, no. 3, September, pp. 304–5

Goldthorpe, J. and Lockwood, D. 1963. 'Affluence and the British class structure',
Sociological Review, vol. 11, no. 2, pp. 133–63

Goldthorpe J., Lockwood, D., Bechofer, H. and Platt, J. 1968A. *The Affluent
Worker: Industrial Attitudes and Behaviour* (Cambridge: CUP)

    1968B. *The Affluent Worker: Political Attitudes and Behaviour* (Cambridge:
CUP)

    1969. *The Affluent Worker in the Class Structure* (Cambridge: CUP)

Gouldner, A.W. 1947. 'Attitudes of 'progressive' trade union Leaders', *AJS* 52,
March, pp. 389–92

Government Social Survey, 1968. *Workplace Industrial Relations* (London, HMSO)

Herberg, W. 1953. 'Bureaucracy and democracy in labour unions', *The Antioch
Review,* Fall, pp. 405–17

Herzberg, H. 1953. 'The old-timers and the newcomers', *Journal of Social
Issues,* vol 9, no. 1, pp. 12–9

Kerr, W.A. 1953. 'Mutual emotional acceptance by union and management'.
Monthly Labor Review, LXXVI, no. 12, December, pp. 1274–6

Kornhauser, A., Sheppard, H.L. and Mayer, A.J. 1956. *When Labor Votes* (New
York: University Books)

Kovner, J., and Lahne, H. J. 1953 'Shop society and the union' *Industrial and
Labour Relations Review,* 7, October, pp. 3–14

Kyllonen, T.E. 1951. 'Social characteristics of active unionists', *AJS,* 56, May, pp. 528–33

Lane, T. and Roberts, K. 1971. *Strike at Pilkingtons* (London: Fontana)

Lipset, S.M., Trow, M.A. and Coleman, J.S. 1956. *Union Democracy* (New York: The Free Press).

Lipset, S.M. and Gordon, J. 1953. 'Mobility and trade union membership', in Bendix, R. and Lipset, S.M. (eds.) *Class, Status and Power* (Glencoe, IL: The Free Press)

Liverpool, University of, Department of Social Science 1954. *The Dockworker* (Liverpool: Liverpool University Press)

Lockwood, D. 1966. 'Sources of variation in working class images of society', *Sociological Review,* vol. 14, no. 3, November pp. 249–67
    1975. 'In search of the traditional worker' in Bulmer, M. (ed) *Working Class Images of Society* (London: Routledge and Kegan Paul)

McCarthy, W.E.J. and Parker, S.R. 1968. *Shop Stewards and Workshop Relations,* Royal Commission on Trade Unions and Employers' Associations, Research Papers 10, (London: HMSO)

MacKenzie, G. 1973. *The Aristocracy of Labour* (Cambridge, CUP)

Mallet, S. 1975. *The New Working Class* (Nottingham: Spokesman Books)

Mann, M. 1973. *Consciousness and Action among the Western Working Class* (London: Macmillan).

Milbrath, L.W. 1972. *Political Participation* (Chicago: Rand McNally).

Miller, G.W. and Young, J.E. 1955 'Membership participation in the trade union local', *American Journal of Economics and Sociology,* 15, October, pp. 31–47

Moore, R. 1975. 'Religion as a source of variation in working-class images of society', in Bulmer, M. (ed.) *Working Class Images of Society* (London: Routledge and Kegan Paul)

Moran, M. 1974. *The Union of Post Office Workers* (London: Macmillan)

Newton, K. 1969. *The Sociology of British Communism* (London: Allen Lane)

Nicholson N. and Ursell, G. 1977. 'The NALGO. activists' *New Society,* vol. 42, no. 793, 15 December, pp. 581–2

Olson, M. 1965. *The Logic of Collective Action* (Cambridge, MA: Harvard University Press)

Parker, S. 1974. *Workplace Industrial Relations 1972* (London: HMSO)
    1975. *Workplace Industrial Relations 1973* (London: HMSO)

Parkin, F. 1971. *Class Inequality and Political Order* (London: MacGibbon and Kee)

Pedler, M. 1973/74. 'Shop stewards as leaders', *Industrial Relations,* Winter vol. 4 no. 4

Poole, M. 1974A. 'Towards a sociology of shop stewards', *The Sociological Review* vol. 22, no. 1, February, pp. 57–82
    1974B. 'What are unions for?' *New Society,* 9 May, vol. 25, no. 605, p. 324

Political and Economic Planning 1948. *British Trade Unionism* (London: HMSO)

Popitz, H., Bahrat, H.P., Jueres, E.A. and Kesting, A. 1969. 'The workers' image of society', in Burns, T., *Industrial Man* (Harmondsworth: Penguin).

Purcell, T. 1953A. *The Worker Speaks his Mind on Company and Union* (Cambridge, Mass.: Havard University Press)
    1953B. 'Dual allegiance at Swift and Co., Chicago' *Monthly Labor Review,* LXXVI, no. 12, December pp. 1276–7

Reiner, R. 1978. *The Blue-Coated Worker* (Cambridge: CUP)

Roberts, B.C. 1956. *Trade Union Government and Administration in Great Britain* (London: Bell)

Rose, A. 1952. *Union Solidarity - The Internal Cohesion of a Labor Union.* (Minneapolis: Univ. of Minnesota Press)

Sayles, L.R. and Strauss, G., 1967. *The Local Union* (New York: Harcourt Brace)

Scott, W.J., Banks, J.A., Halsey, A.H. and Lupton, T. 1956. *Technical Change and Industrial Relations* (Liverpool: Liverpool University Press)

Seidman, J., London, J. and Karsh, B. 1950. Leadership in a Local Union' *AJS* 56, November, pp. 229–37
  1951-2. 'Political consciousness in a local union', *Public Opinion Quarterly,* XV, no. 4, Winter, pp. 692–702

Seidman, J., London, J., Karsh, B. and Tagliacozzo, D. 1958. *The Worker Views his Union* (Chicago: University of Chicago Press)

Shepard, H.A. 1949. 'Democratic control in a labour union', *AJS* 54, January, pp. 311–6

Spinrad, W. 1960. 'Correlates of trade union participation: a summary of the literature' *ASR,* vol. 13, no. 1, pp. 237–244

Strauss, G. and Sayles, L.R. 1952. 'Patterns of participation in local unions', *Industrial and Labour Relations Review,* vol. 6, October, pp. 31–43

Tannenbaum, A.S. 1965. 'Unions' in March, J.G. (ed.), *Handbook of Organizations,* (Chicago: Rand McNally)

Tannenbaum, A.S. and Kahn, R.L. 1958. *Participation in Union Locals* (Evanston, Ill.: Row, Peterson)

Taylor, R. 1974. 'Reds under the bed?', *New Society,* 17 January, vol. 27, no. 589, pp. 119–121

Turner, H.A. 1962. *Trade Union Growth, Structure and Policy* (London: George Allen and Unwin)

Van de Vall, M. 1970. *Labor Organizations* (Cambridge: Cambridge University Press)

Webb, S. and B. 1902. *History of Trade Unionism* (London: Longmans)

Westergaard, J. and Resler, M. 1975. *Class in a Capitalist Society* (London: Heinemann)

Whyte, W.F. 1944. 'Who goes union and why?', *Personnel Journal,* 23, no 6, December, pp. 215–30

Wilensky, H.L. 1956. 'The labor vote: a local union's impact on the political conduct of its members', *Social Forces,* December, 36, pp. 111–120
  1961. 'Life cycle, work situation and participation in formal associations', in Kleemier, R.W. (ed.), *Ageing and Leisure* (New York: OUP)

Zweig, F. 1952. *The British Worker* (Harmondsworth: Penguin)

INDEX

153